Depth Psycho
and Religious Belief

Depth Psychology and Religious Belief

CHRISTOPHER BRYANT

Foreword by Robert F. Hobson

Memoir of Christopher Bryant by David Campbell

Darton, Longman and Todd
London

Published in 1987 by
Darton, Longman and Todd Ltd
89 Lillie Road, London SW6 1UD

First published in 1972 by
Mirfield Publications

© 1985 Mirfield Publications

ISBN 0 232 51763 0

British Library Cataloguing in Publication Data

Bryant, Christopher, *1905–1985*
  Depth psychology and religious belief.
  1. Psychology, Religious
  I. Title
  200'.1'9   BL53

ISBN 0–232–51763–0

Phototypeset by Input Typesetting Ltd, London SW19 8DR
Printed and bound in Great Britain by
Anchor Brendon Ltd, Tiptree, Essex.

Contents

Foreword

'Therefore swink and sweat in all that thou can'st and mayest to get thee a true knowing and feeling of thyself as thou art.' These words of a medieval contemplative Christian express succinctly the aim of the modern psychotherapist and speak to all who wish to live a more abundant life in our modern age.

Father Bryant's knowledge, ideas and experience were developed in four important books. This, his first, is basic to the others and it remains his most direct, lucid, and readable account of fundamentals of depth psychology which are most relevant to the understanding and practice of the religious life.

In its broadest sense 'religion' is concerned with growing up – becoming a *person* more and more able to experience, and to realise in action, the riches of the hidden inner world and of relationships with others. It means not only acquiring intellectual knowledge but also developing a 'true feeling', a language of the heart. In his informed and clear exposition of a complex subject Father Bryant has much to say to the atheist and agnostic as well as to those who profess a religious belief, and his concise account of the principles of depth psychology stands by itself as a reliable introduction to this field of enquiry. But it is in elucidating that difficult area of the relationship of religion and psychology that the long experience and open-mindedness of the skilled spiritual director makes its impact. The practising Christian is shown how psychological insights, far from being undermining, can enrich his faith. Like the author of *The Cloud of Unknowing*, Father Bryant reveals how a true knowing and feeling of oneself can promote a true knowing and feeling of God as he is.

Christopher Bryant *lived* his ideas in humility and love. He was a man of God who, with Irenaeus, believed 'the Glory of God is man fully alive'. I was privileged to be his friend.

Robert F. Hobson

Dr R. F. Hobson is Reader in Psychotherapy, University of Manchester and Training Analyst, Society of Analytical Psychology.

Memoir of
Christopher Bryant SSJE

It was when I was an undergraduate at Oxford shortly before the war that I first stepped across the threshold of the Mission House in east Oxford which was the mother house of the Society of St John the Evangelist, commonly known as the Cowley Fathers. My host was Christopher Bryant, then one of the most junior members. After a rather unappetising lunch this energetic young priest with (according to the prevalent custom) closely cropped hair took me for a walk up Headington Hill. It was difficult for my short legs to keep up with his lengthy strides, and my shyness did not make it easy to converse with this priest wearing a very short cassock, and the old fashioned 'Cowley Father hat'.

With the exception of a short spell in Scotland, Fr Bryant was based in Oxford for nearly twenty-five years. He had a fine voice in those days, and was in charge of the music when SSJE aspired to and reached a very high standard in the rendering of plainsong. He also took a large share in the work of preaching and conducting retreats. All the time he applied himself with great diligence to prayer and wide reading, making a special study of psychology and its relationship with the life of prayer. For a few years he was novice guardian, and then assistant superior.

It was in 1955 that he was appointed to be in charge of St Edward's House, the Society's house in Westminster, and it was from that time that his considerable gifts as a spiritual director began to be recognised. St Edward's House had already existed for fifty years as a centre for retreats as well as for the ministry of spiritual direction and the sacrament of absolution. Christopher, however, took on numerous outside engagements, and in particular gave much time to assisting in the very active West London University Chaplaincy based on the Imperial College of Science. It was a series of lectures given to the students there which formed the basis of the first book he wrote.

He was by this time already an elderly man, and although friends encouraged him he could not obtain a publisher until Mirfield Publications came to the rescue and agreed to publish *Depth Psychology and Religious Belief*. This was to be the first of four books, all written when he was over seventy. The other three books, namely *The River Within*, *The Heart in Pilgrimage* and *Jung and the Christian Way*, are published by Darton, Longman and Todd. Popular as these last three books have been, they have in no way superseded this, his first book, and it is most encouraging that it is possible to produce this new edition.

After Fr Bryant ceased to be in charge of St Edward's House, he was for a short while chaplain to St Augustine's College, Canterbury, at that time a theological college. He also became editor of a popular theological and literary journal, sponsored by SSJE entitled *New Fire*. Every quarter for fifteen years he wrote editorials which have been described as 'little masterpieces of wisdom and shrewd comment'.

During the last six years of his life he returned to reside at St Edward's House. By now he had become widely known for his writings as well as for his conducting of retreats and schools of prayer. This in turn resulted in more and more people seeking his help as a confessor and spiritual director. In fact the last few years of his life were years of most fruitful and busy ministry.

The secret of Christopher Bryant's influence, however, undoubtedly lay in his application to prayer. His day started before the rest of us with a very long period of prayer, and this undoubtedly resulted in an ability to give his full attention to everything he did and to everybody whom he met. On all who knew him, particularly in the last years of his life, he made a deep impression – the impression of an old man who was always youthful in mind, always keen to explore. As the Dean of Salisbury put it in his funeral oration 'he explored the frontiers of human consciousness and the depths of human conflict'. Christ was his master and guide, but much of his exploration was inspired by and was done, as it were, in the company of Carl Jung. For ordinary people, he was surely one of the most outstanding spiritual guides raised up by God in the last decade.

On the morning of 8th June 1985 I saw him off in cheerful holiday mood to visit friends in the country. It was while he was with them that without any warning he suddenly collapsed and died. The very last entry in his private diary, written on the morning of his death, was 'To-day I go to see Terry, Rosslyn and family. The Spirit of Praise'.

'The Spirit of Praise' was the basic secret of Christopher Bryant's youthful exploring vitality which was his to the very last.

St Edward's House   David Campbell
Westminster   Superior-General SSJE
September 1985

Acknowledgements

My thanks are due to the following authors and publishers for permission to use various quotations:

Dr Anthony Storr and William Heinemann Ltd for passages from *The Integrity of the Personality*.

Faber and Faber Ltd for quotations from 'Burnt Norton' from T. S. Eliot's *Collected Poems 1909–1962*.

Penguin Books Ltd for passages from *Dreams and Nightmares* by J. A. Hadfield.

The Revd H. A. Williams, CR, and Constable & Company Ltd, for a passage from *The True Wilderness*.

My thanks are further in an especial degree due to the Community of the Resurrection for undertaking to publish the book, to Dr R. F. Hobson for writing the Foreword* as well as for criticising the first draft of the book, to Dr C. E. Friedlander who at the outset encouraged me to expand the original lectures into a book, and to the Revd Laurie Green who helped me to improve the first draft.

Christopher Bryant SSJE

* Revised for the 1987 edition.

Introduction

Psychology and belief in God

Today many people deny the existence of God and many more who stop short of atheism have serious doubts about it. This book is not concerned with either proving or disproving the truth of this belief, but rather with showing how depth psychology can shed light on the experience of believing. For, true or false, faith in God is a widespread and important experience, worthy of the attention of the agnostic and believer alike. Some may feel uneasy at having the motives underlying their faith scrutinised by the psychologist. They fear that to explain the human element in it may be to explain their faith away. But this need not be so. A child is told that a thunderstorm means that God is angry and later learns with a shock about the electrical origin of thunderstorms. The new knowledge need not destroy his faith in God; rather it might strengthen it by ridding it of the idea that God was capricious like some hot-tempered man. In the same way, though insight into the psychology of belief may come as a disturbing shock to the believer, the shock may well prove salutary and help to free him from childish or superstitious elements in it.

My own standpoint is that of a believer and a Christian who has found his faith deepened by his study of psychology. I do not think that Christians have a monopoly of religious truth, nor that they have not a great deal to learn from other religions. But my examples of religious experience and my account of religious belief will be drawn from the Christian tradition. For Christianity is the only religion I know from within; and to write about a religion one has never practised would be like a book about marriage written

1

by a bachelor. And though the book may lose in breadth by this limitation of its scope it should gain in clarity. I must, however, confess that in my judgement psychology provides no decisive arguments for or against either the existence of God or the truth or falsehood of religious belief. The evidence that psychology has to offer will be interpreted in accordance with the psychologist's prior belief or disbelief. An agnostic may think that by tracing the course by which a firm belief arises he has disproved the belief. The believer, on the other hand, will regard the psychic mechanism of belief as just the way God leads men to put their trust in him.

Freud regarded belief in God as a wish-fulfilment. The frightened child feels safe when father is around. As he grows older and realises that his father cannot be relied upon to help in facing the fears and anxieties that beset him after childhood, he finds the idea of God a reassuring substitute for his father. Jung on the other hand, who at one time shared Freud's standpoint about religion, later came to interpret the phenomena in an opposite sense. As a result of trying to understand his patients and help them to solve their problems, he came to think that the tendency to believe in God, what he called the God archetype, is innate in man. The tendency leads men to make absolutes, to give unconditional value, if not to God then to an ideal, a person or a cause, in other words to make gods of these things. The infant, for example, tends to make gods of his father and mother and to think of them as all-wise and all-powerful, like gods. Thus Freud and Jung came to diametrically opposite conclusions from the same psychological data. For Freud God is a father-substitute, for Jung a child's father is a God-substitute.

To take another example of the same psychological facts being given opposite interpretations, it is sometimes said that the effectiveness of prayer is due entirely to autosuggestion. Now while it is undoubtedly true that autosuggestion is at work when a person prays as in a great many other mental activities, it is no less true that autosuggestion itself can be interpreted as a veiled and unacknowledged prayer. When, for example, someone repeats to himself the autosuggestion formula 'every day and in every way I am getting better and

2

better' the words used imply that there is something in the nature of things that will tend to his improvement if only he will trust himself to it. This looks remarkably like a concealed and unconscious reliance on the power of God immanent in the universe and so a kind of prayer. Thus the beneficial effects of autosuggestion, which the unbeliever uses to account for the help people claim to gain from prayer, will be seen by the Christian believer as confirmatory evidence of the importance Christ attached to prayer made with faith. Indeed autosuggestion may indicate to the believer ways of improving his prayer. The techniques of Yoga, especially the breathing methods and the postures, are ways of fostering relaxation, which renders a man more open to autosuggestion and so more able to concentrate on a word or symbol. Though the techniques of Yoga were developed in India, Christians and others have made use of them as a preparation for meditation and prayer.

While it is not within the competence of psychology either to prove or disprove the existence of God, it can shed much light on the experience of believing and can provide some of the evidence to be weighed and sifted by those who try to make up their minds as to the reality of God. It can also help to distinguish healthy from unhealthy forms of faith and so can be of service to those who believe and those who doubt. If it cannot prove the truth of religion it can certainly demonstrate its importance.

Depth psychology

This book approaches the study of religious belief from the direction of depth (or dynamic) psychology rather than that of experimental psychology. Experimental psychology observes and measures human behaviour. It looks at man from the outside and has amassed much information about the way people behave. It has acquired much new knowledge, especially in the sphere of perception, memory and learning. The behaviour of dogs, rats and monkeys has been intensively studied in carefully controlled experiments in order to discover laws of behaviour applicable to man. The experimental psychologist does a great deal of his work in

3

laboratories in which particular emotions such as fear and aggression can be more or less separately aroused and studied and the conclusions statistically expressed. Much of the information, however, that experimental psychology has provided is based on an artificial situation which is far removed from ordinary life.[1]

Depth psychology studies the person as a whole and in his actual life. Its hypotheses or theories are extremely difficult to substantiate because of the virtual impossibility of framing an experiment that would not fatally interfere with the facts which it was attempting to measure. The theories are formulated to account for observed phenomena and are retained, though they may be incapable of scientific proof, because they are believed to explain some areas of mental life better than any other. The great pioneer was the Austrian doctor, Sigmund Freud, who around the turn of the century built up his system, psychoanalysis, from his reflections on the reports of disturbed patients. Other great names are Carl Jung and Alfred Adler, both of whom collaborated with Freud for a time and later broke away to form systems of their own. Since then Klein, Fairbairn and many others have modified the older systems and developed new ones. But beneath the differences in the various schools there is a great deal that they hold in common; and it is with this common ground that I shall be principally concerned in this book. They all, for example, assume the reality of the unconscious and the importance of unconscious fears and wishes for our conscious thinking and behaviour.[2]

To sum up the difference between experimental and depth psychology, the former is based on the scientific observation and analysis of behaviour, the latter on the observation of and reflection on experience. The experimental psychologist looks at a man from the outside, the depth psychologist from

[1] For a readable account of experimental psychology see the trilogy by H. J. Eysenck, *Uses and Abuses of Psychology*, *Sense and Nonsense in Psychology*, *Fact and Fiction in Psychology*, all published by Penguin. For a general history of all the schools of psychology see G. A. Miller, *Psychology: the Science of Mental Life*, Penguin 1970.

[2] For an account of the various schools of depth psychology see J. A. C. Brown, *Freud and the Post-Freudians*, Penguin 1969.

within – or at least from the reports that people make of their thoughts, feelings and wishes, checked and authenticated by his own self-scrutiny. A person's motives are important as well as his conduct. Experimental psychology approximates more closely to the methods of natural science, depth psychology is closer to philosophy. This book approaches religious belief from the direction of depth psychology because it is concerned to understand and evaluate the experience of believing.

I shall avoid as far as possible the use of technical language and where I use such terms as the *ego*, the *unconscious* and *repression* I shall generally be using them in a somewhat imprecise and non-technical sense. I do this partly because psychologists of different schools do not use them with exactly the same meaning. But I do it also in order to avoid giving the impression that the words correspond to clearly known facts. They are not unlike the sixteenth-century maps of Africa which indicate the fact of the African continent but are not to be relied on in detail. Statements occur on a large-scale map such as 'here are lions' or 'here is the great swamp', which are powerful in their appeal to the imagination and are unquestionably founded on fact but are too vague to be useful as a traveller's guide. In any case this popular use of words will better serve my purpose, which is not to expound any particular theory of depth psychology but to use its ideas and insights to shed light on religious belief.

In this book I shall make considerable use of the ideas of Carl Jung, who as a religious man has much more to say about religion than Freud, an atheist who regarded religion as an illusion though, like art, an important illusion. Jung on the other hand has recorded that of the patients who came to him for psychological treatment in middle life (he specifically excepts the young) every one had fallen ill because he lacked what the living religions of all ages have given to their adherents. He added that they never got well unless and until they acquired or recovered a religious attitude to life. He did not refer to their necessarily becoming Christians nor indeed to their becoming practising members of any religious body. He meant the gaining of an attitude of reverence or humility

towards a reality greater than themselves.[3] Jung attempted
to describe and explain areas of experience with which few
other psychologists have concerned themselves. Some of his
theories have been criticised as fanciful; but they were framed
to shed light on important facts and it is possible to learn a
great deal from his insights without subscribing to all his
brilliant guesses.

In chapter 1 I shall give some account of man as pictured
by the depth psychologist, who looks behind man's behaviour and visible achievements to his inner motives and
unconscious fears and wishes. In chapter 2 I shall try to let
this picture illuminate man's experience of God. I shall try
to indicate the human element in avowed religious experience and the religious element in experience common to all
men whether they acknowledge it as such or not. In chapter
3 I shall describe the part that faith plays in enabling a person
to realise to the full his potential as a human being. As I
criticise some forms of faith as unhealthy I shall in a final
chapter describe in outline the kind of Christian belief which
can stand up to the criticisms of the psychologists.

[3] See C. G. Jung, *Modern Man in Search of a Soul* (Kegan Paul 1936), p. 264.

1

Depth psychology and the understanding of man

The unconscious: memory

A characteristic of depth psychology, from which it derives its name, is the important place it gives to the unconscious in the understanding of man; and some illustrations of the fact of the unconscious will make a good introduction to our subject. Consider memory. You are asked the name of the author of a book you read recently; you try hard to remember but the name escapes you. Then, perhaps an hour later when you are thinking of something else, the name suddenly pops up in your mind. Where was the name when you were trying to remember it? It was not in your consciousness and we can only say that it was unconscious. It is as though it was stored somewhere below the floor of consciousness in the cellars of the unconscious, and the effort to remember instigates a search through its files. It is believed that the memory of all past experiences is recorded in some region whether of the mind or the brain, some of it easily accessible, some of it accessible only with difficulty, some of it inaccessible to any ordinary effort. Though memory is by no means fully understood it probably has a physical basis. Certainly brain injury can damage memory. Perhaps it is analogous to sounds recorded on tape. The sounds are not actually on the tape but only the possibility of reviving them. We can suppose that similarly there are impressed on the brain recordings of past experience, some faint, some strong and vivid. Given the right stimulus the recording is played over in the light of consciousness.

Some psychologists distinguish between the unconscious and the preconscious. The preconscious includes both facts which you know well and don't happen to be thinking of, such as your home address or your birthday, and facts which you have temporarily forgotten but could recall in time. The unconscious includes facts which you appear to have forgotten completely and cannot recall by any deliberate effort, but which nevertheless may sometimes be brought back into consciousness in the train of some picture, word or sound which is in some way associated with the forgotten memory. But however we define the unconscious, the experience of memory is evidence that there is a great deal in the mind of which we are unaware.

The unconscious: post-hypnotic suggestion

But the unconscious is not only a store house of memory; it contains also a large number of instinctive tendencies, some of which we notice when we turn our attention to them and others which we know only through their effects. That a man can have impulses and tendencies within him which, unknown to him, affect his conduct is very simply illustrated by the phenomenon of post-hypnotic suggestion. Hypnosis is an imperfectly understood state in which a man's critical faculties appear to be asleep and he will accept unquestioningly the suggestions that the hypnotist makes to him. A man is hypnotised and told that when he hears the clock strike he will put on his overcoat. He is then informed that he will forget being told to do this and is awakened from hypnosis. Presently the clock strikes, he gets up, makes some excuse about feeling cold, fetches his overcoat and puts it on. He is quite unaware of the real reason for his action, which is a tendency implanted by the hypnotist. Professor Eysenck tells a story of a psychologist, a man of strong will and personality, who sometimes made use of hypnosis. He arranged to be hypnotised himself so that he might experience it from the receiving end. He was hypnotised and then told that at a given signal he would get up from his place in the circle and cross over to a chair on the opposite side. He was awakened from hypnosis and later the signal was given. He was observed to fidget for a few moments. Then he said 'I have a strong urge to cross over to that chair. You must have told me to do it under hypnosis, but I'm damned if I will.' He sat restless in his chair for a few minutes; then he got up saying, 'I can't stand it any longer', crossed the room and sat down in the chair indicated. In this case the tendency implanted in him was so strong that though he guessed its origin it gave him no peace until he had obeyed it.

Hypnosis, though derived from a Greek word meaning sleep and resembling sleep in certain respects, is not true sleep. A person who allows himself to be hypnotised becomes very open to suggestions made by the hypnotist which, unless they are contrary to some strongly held principle, he will accept uncritically and completely. Hypnosis is sometimes used in place of an anaesthetic before an operation or before child-birth. The patient is hypnotised and told that the operation will be painless and sure enough he feels no pain.[1]

The unconscious: mental illness

Post-hypnotic suggestion is an artificial example of the impulses and tendencies which occur in us in the ordinary course of life and, unknown to us, influence our conscious thoughts, feelings and actions. A great deal otherwise unaccountable in our behaviour is due to the interference of these inner forces. Freud in the *Psychopathology of Everyday Life*[2] gives innumerable instances of mistakes – forgetting well known names, slips of the tongue and pen, bungled actions, losing or mislaying things – apparently accidental but in reality due to some unconscious cause. In case after case Freud provides a plausible reason for the mistake in some painful forgotten memory or unacknowledged fear. He has said that the things we forget are the things we have some secret reason for wanting to forget. A careful analysis of the things you have forgotten recently will probably convince you that there is at least some truth in the saying. The extreme case of mental illness can often shed light on the problems of normal people. Professor Grensted writes of an

[1] See H. J. Eysenck, *Sense and Nonsense in Psychology* (Penguin 1970), ch. 1.
[2] Penguin 1975; see chapters 3 and 8.

account, published in a medical journal, of one of the doctor's cases. The doctor's patient suffered from the delusion that he was a dog. The account described the symptoms, outlined the treatment and finally claimed a complete cure. But there was a footnote to the report which ran 'unfortunately the patient now believes he is a water-rat'. The doctor had successfully treated the symptoms while leaving the underlying cause intact, with the result that the deepdown cause, presumably after an interval, produced further and possibly more embarrassing symptoms. Often a person is unable to break some habit of which he disapproves, because the habit is itself the symptom of something hidden in the unconscious. Until the underlying cause has been discovered and faced, the symptoms will persist.[3]

The unconscious: dreams

The best of all illustrations of unconscious mental activity is the dream, which can be termed the activity of the mind during sleep. The mind goes on working during sleep at the unsolved problems of waking life. Most people have had the experience on waking of having found the solution of a problem that had been on their minds the day before. They have discovered for themselves the value of the advice, 'Sleep on it'. The dream is the language of the unconscious, a pictorial language often hard to decipher. The picture language of a dream often resembles that of a political cartoon, in which you may see depicted a mounted knight in armour charging with levelled lance a smoke-breathing dragon. Then you notice that the face of the knight resembles that of the chancellor of the exchequer and you see printed on the dragon the words 'wage inflation' or 'devaluation'. Dreams are seldom so easy to interpret as such a cartoon and the actors in a dream drama do not often have labels attached. Very often the characters in a dream represent

[3] It is not always true that to cure a symptom you must discover and deal with the underlying cause. Sometimes the symptom is just a habit whose original cause is no longer operative or is only very weak. In such cases when the symptom is cured it does not recur nor give place to another symptom.

aspects of the dreamer's own personality, and it is notoriously difficult to recognise one's own weaknesses. But the analogies drawn from some incident whether of everyday life or of legend which the cartoonist uses to shed light on a contemporary situation resemble closely the symbolism of dreams. The images of a dream are often borrowed from the dreamer's recent past but are used in the way a cartoonist uses them to illuminate some problem pressing for solution in the dreamer's own life.

The dream was called by Freud the royal road to the unconscious and something further must be said about a subject interesting in itself, which depth psychology had used in building up its picture of man. As a working hypothesis I shall follow what J. A. Hadfield, has called 'the biological theory of dreams'. According to this theory the dream 'by reproducing the unsolved experiences of life works towards the solution of these problems'. This theory accepts some of the principles of dream interpretation laid down by Freud and incorporates a great deal of Jung's theories about the dream within a simpler hypothesis. There are as many types of dream as there are of conversation. Three illustrations must suffice.

The first I take from Hadfield's book:

A lady was driving a car, and, feeling for her handkerchief, changed her right hand to the left side of the steering wheel. She swerved, ran on to the path of the country road and narrowly missed landing in the ditch, but righted herself in time. After a moment's fright she made light of it, no doubt to excuse her foolishness. That night she dreams of the car swerving, but in the dream it drives across the road, down the steep bank beyond, and is completely wrecked. That was not what happened but what might have happened. Moreover the dream enforced this on her the more vividly by making her relive it. In the day she makes light of it because she dislikes being reminded of her foolishness: her dream . . . reverts to the incident and compels her to face up to the situation by emphasising the possible consequencies of her carelessness – an idea that she conveniently repressed. The terror of this

11

dream had the effect of making her much more cautious, whereas the experience of the day failed to do so: it was a corrective to her false optimism.[4]

That is an example of a warning dream. I will give one of Jung's dreams to illustrate the problem-solving dream. Jung has described how once he was making very little progress with a woman patient. They were approaching a point of mutual frustration and the possible breaking off of the treatment. Then Jung dreamt that the patient, much larger than life, was standing on top of a building so high that he had to crane his neck to look at her. On waking he drew the conclusion that the dream was telling him that he had been grossly underestimating his patient and that he needed to look up to her. At the next session with his patient he recounted the dream together with his interpretation of it. After that they got on famously. The dream helped him to solve the problem with his patient that had been worrying him. His unconscious was aware of the facts which his conscious mind had overlooked, and by means of a dream helped him to correct the unduly low opinion of his patient that threatened to wreck the treatment.

My third illustration I will take from the Bible: St Peter's dream while staying at the sea-port town of Joppa, as given in the Acts of the Apostles (ch. 10). Hungry and waiting for dinner Peter fell asleep on the flat roof of the house and dreams of a great sheet, like a ship's sail, lowered from heaven. On the sheet were a great number of birds and beasts reckoned unclean by the Jewish law and forbidden as food for Jews. A voice addresses him, 'Rise Peter, kill and eat.' He answers, 'No Lord, I have never eaten anything common or unclean.' The voice replies, 'You must not call common or unclean what God has made clean.' The dream was repeated a second and then a third time. The sequel is well known, the sudden arrival of messengers from a Gentile centurion, Cornelius by name, who had himself been directed in a dream to send for Peter and had been given detailed directions how to find him. In response to the request Peter went with the messenger to the centurion's

[4] J. A. Hadfield, *Dreams and Nightmares* (Penguin 1973), pp. 70–1.

home at Caesarea where he preached to the Gentiles present and afterwards baptised them. The images of Peter's dream were drawn from recent experience. He was hungry and dreamt about food. As a fisherman he would have noted with interest ships sailing in and out of the harbour at Joppa and in his dream he sees a sail descending. The dream was apparently to do with Jewish food regulations which must have been of some concern to a Jew who travelled about as did Peter; but actually it dealt with a burning issue for Christians at that time. For the first Christians were all Jews and to many the Christians were just a slightly unorthodox Jewish sect. The question at issue was this: must all Gentiles who wished to become Christians become Jews at the same time and undergo the rite of circumcision? The dream was telling Peter that he must not think Gentiles unclean and so to be excluded from the Christian Church till they had been circumcised. Through his unconscious, addressing him in the symbolic language of a dream, Peter, and through him the Christian Church was led to face and solve the problem. The fact that the story is told twice in Acts points to the importance that was attached to it then.

The unity of consciousness and the unconscious

Though some people claim never or very rarely to dream, experiments have shown that all people do dream and that the dreams we remember are only a small part of our total dreaming. Further depth psychology sees man's mental life as a single interconnected whole, partly conscious, partly unconscious. Man has been likened to an iceberg, the part above the surface corresponding to his conscious mind, the under-water part to the unconscious. The drift of the iceberg will be determined not only by the winds which play upon its upper regions but also and perhaps even more by the currents that tug it down below. The whole of what a man is, both what he is conscious of and his unconscious, works together as a single unit. A man's conscious and deliberate acts often cause repercussions in the unconscious that work against his avowed intentions.

The analogy of the iceberg illustrates the unity of the

13

personality but in no way indicates the dynamism of man; nor does it suggest the importance of consciousness, a crucial element in the personality. An iceberg drifts according to the pull of the current and the strength of the wind. The human personality is self-directing. A person responds to society around him and the world in which he finds himself partly by conscious reflection and decision. This conscious, directing element in a person is called the ego. But the ego is not only concerned with responding to other people, it also has a ruling function within the whole personality, including the unconscious. The conscious personality, the ego, may be compared to the king of a country in the days when kings were effective rulers. A tyrannical king was a misfortune to a country, and tended to make his people discontented and rebellious. But a weak king was a disaster. He was at the mercy of strong men and favourites. Lawlessness, anarchy or civil war were likely to break out where a weak king ruled over a country with no strong tradition of law and order. The ideal king would be strong enough to be in touch with his people at every point and open to all the currents of thought and the pressures of particular interests and yet, though sensitive to these influences, able to stand up to them and to reign. So a man's conscious personality, his ego, should as much as possible be aware of and open to the pressures from the unconscious, should be influenced by them, but should be in control.

Repression

Our problems, of course, are not wholly within ourselves. We are all our lives dependent on others and our inner difficulties are bound up with difficulties with other people. It is often because a person is pulled two ways by inner problems that he finds his domestic situation intolerable. But equally a nagging wife or family or bad accommodation may increase a person's inner tensions to explosion point. We are not at all like kings who have no concern except with ruling their own kingdoms; we are like kings surrounded by other countries each with its own ruler. Indeed to begin with and for many years we are less like a sovereign state than a colony

14

ruled over by parents or guardians. Only bit by bit do we become independent enough to exercise full self-government. Personal problems are directly or indirectly intertwined with problems concerning others.

We shall come back to the subject of inter-personal relationships in chapter 3. We must now consider some of the happenings that lead to inward division and frustration. Both in relation to others and within ourselves things go wrong largely through fear. A child has an experience which because of his ignorance and weakness he finds terrifying: he thinks he is lost and abandoned, he is bullied or ridiculed by older children, he is badly frightened by a dog. He cannot bear to think about it; he pushes it out of his mind and succeeds in forgetting it. He is helped in this by his ability to live in a world of dream and fantasy. He appears to have got rid of his fear but he has not really done so. He has sealed it off from his consciousness, but the repressed fear within him is far from dead. It lives on in a heightened tendency to be frightened or to fear anything resembling the painful experience. It will, if it is at all strong, hinder and distort his growth until it has been brought to light and faced. This kind of thing takes place in everyone. There is an instinctive tendency to repress a disagreeable experience; not to do so may make life unbearable, especially in childhood. It is perhaps the best we can do to cope with an intolerable situation. Nevertheless, it is an evasion, a running away from reality, from something that must be faced if life is not to be cramped and stunted. It is as though a king were afraid to face a disagreeable section of his people and banished it from his mind. The obnoxious element in the population will remain to give trouble, all the more for being ignored.

Repression in the strict sense means pushing the painful memory right out of the consciousness. Its mechanism is unconscious and indeliberate. The man who has repressed a painful experience has forgotten it completely. Repression differs from suppression in which a man is well aware of the painful experience but deliberately chooses not to dwell on it. Suppression is a far healthier way of dealing with unpleasant memories than repression. But in practice repression is seldom complete and what often happens is a mixture of

15

repression and suppression, in which the unbearable experience is largely but not wholly forgotten. In this book I shall use 'repression' to refer not only to complete repression but also to the case where the painful experience is partly repressed by a fear which prevents it from becoming fully conscious and partly kept under deliberately.

Some commonly repressed feelings: (1) Fear

One of the emotions that is commonly found unbearable, and so repressed, is fear itself. Fear is necessary to our survival in an unsafe world. It is a motor-horn to warn us of danger. Mild fear is not always disagreeable and can add a pleasing spice of excitement to relieve monotony. But acute fear is extremely painful; and if I cannot escape from the frightening situation or change it I shall probably try to anaesthetise myself to it by driving it out of my mind. My great aim will be make myself feel secure. Two attitudes are commonly adopted to keep the dreaded pain of being afraid out of consciousness. One is the active devil-may-care attitude of the man who takes risks recklessly. The other is the passive obstinate unflappability of the man who equally refuses to admit the reality of danger. When the cracks in the wall are growing noticeably bigger such a man will reply to those who point this out, 'Don't worry, everything will be all right.' Both these attitudes must be distinguished from true courage. The genuinely brave man sees and feels danger, yet takes the risks that occasion demands and keeps calm despite his fears. The man whose fear is deeply repressed has developed the habit of refusing to see danger. He fails to realise that sensitivity to danger is an asset provided that it does not overwhelm him. The more conscious he is of the forces that threaten his existence or way of life, or the people or causes he values, the more all his faculties will be alerted to counter the danger. The person we are thinking of would rather live in a fool's paradise than face unpleasant facts. He is more anxious to avoid feeling afraid than to overcome the causes of fear.

During war when men undergo extreme danger the repression of acute fear sometimes leads to bodily symptoms in a man which he is powerless to control. A man physically uninjured by a shell exploding near him represses the momentary terror because it does not square with his ideal of himself as a brave man. But the repressed terror active within the man paralyses him and he finds himself unable to move his limbs. He is paralysed not by a physical wound but by fear. Many other symptoms of shell-shock are due to repressed fear. Sometimes a person represses the natural fear of death. Because he won't face the fact of death he is reluctant to see a doctor about symptoms which might mean that he was suffering from a fatal disease. If he would admit to himself the possibility of this he would go at once to a doctor. Very likely his fears would prove groundless, but even though they should prove well founded the earlier he received medical attention the greater his chance of recovery. Thus the represented fear of death can lead a person to fly in the face of commonsense and hasten the thing he is afraid of.

(2) *The feeling of worthlessness*

Another feeling we would all be rid of if we could is the feeling of worthlessness, of inferiority. Everyone has had in childhood the experience of being made to feel small, to feel unwanted, to feel nobody. This is a demoralising as well as a painful feeling. For there is a right and true self-esteem which gives a man the inner security he needs if he is to value others rightly. We can only gain this healthy self-esteem from realising that other people value us. A pupil needs some encouragement if he is to do the work of which he is capable. If he feels he is no good he will lack the incentive to give of his best. When a person in old age ceases to have others dependent on him he often begins to feel useless; and the loss of self-esteem which makes him more anxious about himself renders him less genial and considerate to others. The inertia of the drug addict and his weakened sense of obligation to others is not only due to the direct effect of the drug but to the loss of self-esteem. To feel utterly worthless is not only painful but undermines a person's concern for

17

other people and the general good. A certain self-esteem is a necessary basis for altruism.[5]

The great reassurance of the child made to feel no good is the certainty of his parents' love. But if this is lacking or the feeling of worthlessness is rubbed in too hard it becomes unbearable and he represses it if he can. It seems and perhaps really is necessary to do so, for a sense of utter uselessness can paralyse effort and cripple achievement. Thus we are driven to build up a mental attitude which will keep this painful feeling shut away out of sight. The attitude that does this best is a dominating and aggressive one. We feel an urge to assert ourselves, to criticise others, to take them down a peg. We are driven to do this by the urgent desire to keep out of mind the painful memory of our own past humiliations. This attitude of self-assertiveness must not be confused with the right and proper self-affirmation of the genuinely mature person. Such a person possesses the right self-esteem that enables him to face his limitations realistically but without worrying about them and so is free from the need to assert himself just in order to prove he is somebody. The mature man can wield authority and act decisively without belittling those around him. The man with repressed feelings of inferiority asserts himself in order to gain the self-esteem that deep down he lacks. It looks as though we can see the workings of repressed feelings of inferiority in the lives of some of the dictators who have brought war on the world. Hitler, the obscure Austrian house painter, struggled first to become the leader of a party, then of Germany and finally, but unsuccessfully, of the world. Mussolini, the Italian contemporary of Hitler, like Napoleon a very short man, declared that he had an insatiable ambition for power. Of course no one becomes a dictator without a great deal of innate ability. But it looks as though some of the driving power behind the achievements of all three dictators came from the need to escape from a painful sense of inferiority.

[5] This psychological truth gives added meaning to the teaching of the Bible that a man should love his neighbour as himself. Unless he has a certain love and esteem for himself he will not be able to love his neighbour.

(3) Rage

A third often repressed emotion is rage. Babies, as everyone knows, are apt to want things passionately and at once, and if thwarted in their wishes are liable to erupt into rage. Not every mother is able to tolerate this rage especially when it is directed, as it often is, at her. Some mothers feel their own anger aroused by the baby's tantrums, and the baby, sensing this, begins to fear that his anger may cost him the love of his mother on whom he knows he utterly depends, however angry he may sometimes be with her. The anger seems to break out compulsively and the child gets frightened of the raging, murderous force within that seems to take possession of him and, he fears, may make his parents reject him. This is the kind of account that child experts give of the origin in many people of the fear of their own anger. Society in general strongly disapproves of openly expressed rage and has ways, such as ridicule, of punishing it. This reinforces the fear of his anger that a child acquired in infancy and strengthens his tendency to repress it. The attitude which best helps to keep aggressive feelings under is that of mild, unprovocative inoffensiveness. There is something not quite natural about the gentle attitude which is adopted, perhaps quite unconsciously, as a defence against repressed anger and aggressiveness. There is a strength behind the truly gentle person, while there is something exasperating about this imitation meekness. For a certain aggressiveness, a fighting spirit is proper to man; and if through fear a person bottles up this fighting potential he will be unable to face people and situations in a fully human way. Unbridled aggression can be extremely destructive, but aggression under control supplies the driving power within such qualities as courage, patience and perseverance.

An example from fiction of aggressiveness concealed under a mask of meekness is Uriah Heap in *David Copperfield* with his constant assertion of his humility, combined with a keen eye on the main chance. Gandhi, who contributed more than any other single individual to the granting of independence to India by the British government, is an example of the strength behind a man of truly gentle character. No one without a great deal of fighting spirit could have worked with the patience and perseverance that he exhibited towards the goal of self-government for India.

(4) Guilt

A fourth feeling liable to be repressed is that of guilt. There is a healthy sense of guilt which a person feels after some wrong action or piece of neglect, a guilt which spurs him to repair the harm he has done and to change his conduct. And there is an unhealthy guilt feeling which is out of all proportion to a man's actual misdeeds and leads to no change for the better. More will be said about this in chapter 2. Both these kinds of guilt have their origin in the tendency of small children to identify with their parents and take over uncriticised their parents' attitudes. So a child will identify with his mother's disapproval of something he has done and will feel ashamed of it. The more attached he is to his mother the greater the feeling of shame. To some extent almost everyone experiences this; but with some children the feeling of guilt is so acute as to become unbearable. They try to suppress it; and the attitude that best helps them to do this is that of self-righteousness, the holier-than-thou attitude. If I make it my great aim to be better than other people, I may manage to attain a sense of moral superiority which will banish the feeling of guilt from my mind. For the sake of this I may be prepared to renounce a great deal. The attitude of the good man in the parable who thanked God for his superior virtue and boasted of his self-denial and large gifts to charity is typical of a man with a repressed sense of guilt. Because he fears deep down that he is bad he attempts to exorcise his fear by going to an extreme of virtue. It is not his conduct that the parable criticises but his motive. His good actions are done neither for love of God nor man but in order to quieten his feeling of guilt.

The contest in unselfishness between two persons, sometimes pushed to ridiculous extremes may betray in each of them the pressure of repressed guilt feelings. It begins with the polite offer of each party to fall in with the other's wishes. 'Would you like to have tea in the garden?' 'Just whatever you wish.' 'But I want to do whatever you would like.' 'But it's all the same to me, do what you would prefer.' The pressure of repressed guilt is betrayed by the unwillingness of either to seem less unselfish than the other. The prize of victory in this game is the smug satisfaction of moral superiority. The repression of guilt is also betrayed by the feelings of self-reproach that sometimes sweep over the close relative of someone who has died. The feelings were kept under while the relative was alive, but bereavement weakens the ego's defences against the feeling of guilt for not having treated one's dead relative as considerately and kindly as one should.

The effects of repression

Earlier I compared the conscious ego in relation to the rest of the personality to a king in relation to his country. Returning to this analogy the painful feelings which we tend to repress are like elements in the population which a king regards as a threat to his reign. A king who had to use troops or armed police to control troublesome elements in his kingdom would be much weakened in his foreign policy. He would hesitate to risk a war which would be bound to expose his inner weakness. Equally when we keep a good deal of our personality bottled up because of painful past experience we are much less able to respond to other people and carry out our duties and responsibilities. Indeed the more completely a man is able to accept the whole of himself, the more he is able to be open to and tolerant of other people. The more a person is on the defensive against elements in his own personality the more he will be on guard against others. Sometimes if the pressure of work and the demands of other people are great he may be unable to withstand the pressure from within and will have a nervous breakdown. Nature thus compels him to terms with his inner problems by making it impossible for him to carry on his normal life. Such a breakdown, by forcing him to face his inner difficulties, can often prove a blessing in disguise. It is as though an outbreak of civil rebellion in a country at war compels its government to break off hostilities with the foreign enemy and sue for peace, as the Bolsheviks did in 1917, when the October revolution brought them to power in Russia during the First World War.

In the interests of clarity I have greatly over-simplified a complex subject. There are degrees of repression and correspondingly there are degrees of unawareness of the emotional storms and explosions that disturb a man within. A person may be totally unconscious of his repressed anger and think that he is not angry at all, though the telltale signs of anger are plain for all to see. But he is more likely to be partly aware of it, though not at all realising its strength and not giving much thought to it; or he may be aware of his anger intermittently. Again the man with the typical inferiority complex does not feel himself inferior at all; he does not allow himself to feel that; he feels superior. His feelings of inferiority are so deeply repressed that he is aware of them only through their effects in a compelling urge to dominate other people. But much more commonly a person is partly or occasionally aware of feelings of insignificance. He has not been able to repress them completely.

We considered earlier the constant interaction of consciousness and the unconscious. Indeed, Jung regards the personality as a self-regulating psychic mechanism with the unconscious as a balancing, compensating force which corrects the one-sidedness of the conscious ego. In some ways it resembles a thermostat which maintains the temperature of a room in winter at, say, 65 degrees Fahrenheit (18°C) by means of a device which causes heat to be switched on directly the temperature drops below 65, and switches it off when it rises above that temperature. The body is itself an amazingly complex and sensitive thermostat which maintains a temperature of 98.4 (36.9°C) with only minor variations in hot weather and cold, and if through some infection it fails, and a man's temperature rises only a degree or two above normal, he at once begins to feel ill. Something like this self-regulating arrangement occurs in the personality. A man tries to bring the whole of himself into line with his deliberate aims and choices. But if his conscious policy clashes with his unconscious fears and wishes, the unconscious will react by forcibly interfering with his aims. The harder a man tries to

22

impose his will on a resisting unconscious the more strongly the unconscious will react, just as the harder you throw a rubber ball on the ground the higher it will bounce. Many people have discovered in war-time that if during an air-raid or a bombardment they tried to repress their fear, by refusing to admit to themselves that they could be afraid, it came back more strongly, while if they acknowledged their fear it became much more controllable.

It is claimed that a good deal of delinquency is partly due to a repressed sense of guilt which drives people to do something to justify their guilt feeling. A feeling of guilt which a man has succeeded in repressing perhaps with the aid of a high moral ideal, pushes him into doing something that he is forced to admit is wrong. Thus the repressed feeling of guilt forces its way into consciousness and compels recognition. I have heard a psychiatrist argue in favour of a particular form of confession in a church service which had been criticised for its exaggerated expressions of sinfulness, on the grounds that it enabled people to give vent to their deep down sense of guilt. If the form of confession were abolished or changed to one that did not allow men to express their sense of guilt adequately, they would be more likely to do wrong. St Augustine, that acute psychologist of the ancient world, described in his *Confessions* his feelings when robbing an orchard as a boy with a gang of his friends. What gave the exploit its thrill and delight was the knowledge that it was forbidden. It was the giving conscious rein to unconscious guilt that made the adventure enjoyable, even though he later came to blame himself severely for his conduct. Again, sometimes a man's deeply repressed fear will egg him on without realising it into a situation so alarming as to break down all his defences against being frightened, so that he becomes badly afraid. Sometimes repressed feelings of worthlessness that a man normally keeps under will sweep over him in the shape of a black mood that he can no more get rid of than he can disperse a London fog.

23

Reaction formations

I have described various attitudes that a person may adopt in order to keep painful feelings out of his mind. These attitudes are themselves defensive reactions to the pressure from the unconscious and have been termed by Freud *reaction formations*. The stronger the repression the stronger will be the reaction formation. They tend to be the diametrical opposite of the feeling that provokes them, both contradicting and balancing them. Thus fear is both balanced and contradicted by an apparently unafraid attitude, the feeling of inferiority by one of superiority, anger by an attitude of mildness, guilt by one of self-righteousness. There are other feelings that are repressed besides those already mentioned, affection for instance. Sometimes the fear of affection can arise in infancy. Babies are normally affectionate and like being cuddled. Sometimes they make demands on their mother's affection which the mother cannot meet. They are badly hurt by being rebuffed and can become afraid of the affectionate feelings which have caused them so much pain. A child may also become afraid of affection for the opposite reason, that his somewhat possessive mother tried to give him more affection than he was ready for, and so brought about a fear and distaste for undue affection. These are some of many ways in which a child in infancy or later may come to be afraid of his affection and to repress it. The attitude that best keeps affection under is a cold, aloof manner that keeps people at a distance. Sex feelings, though not the same as affection, are commonly linked with it. These too are often repressed, partly through social pressure, partly because sex is sometimes mistakenly thought to be unclean. But however it comes about, sex and sex feelings are often feared and repressed. The kind of attitude that best does this is the falsely spiritual one that despises sexuality and is disgusted at the visible expressions of it. The deep interest which Mrs Grundy and those like her show in scandals and love affairs, of which they profess to disapprove, is an indication of the strength of their own sex desire.

The reaction formations unconsciously designed to keep under the feelings we fear become very much part of our

24

character and exceedingly difficult to change. If my affection is bottled up by buried memories of embarrassing experiences in the past, I may try hard to show friendliness to others only to find myself totally unable to discard an aloof and seemingly cold manner which puts people off. The strength of these reaction formations is partly that of habit; for any attitude maintained for some time will acquire a certain strength and durability. But in addition to habit and more powerful in maintaining it is fear, perhaps completely unconscious, of the feeling the attitude was designed to repress.

Projection

An attitude is adopted partly in order to keep under a painful memory but partly also in order to maintain a front to the world. Mrs Brown has developed a dominating and managing manner not only to conceal from herself her deep down feeling of inadequacy but in order to impress Mrs Jones and to prevent her from seeing it too. Thus our reaction formations are caused not only by the fear of a painful emotion but by the pressure of public opinion. Indeed, it is the need to adapt ourselves to others that makes us fear to express openly some of the feelings we repress. We shall return to this interrelation with others in chapter 5. It is mentioned here because it helps to explain the phenomenon called projection, which is one of the ways that repressed feelings reveal themselves.

If I suffer from repressed anxiety I am likely to get very irritated with someone who seems to me over-anxious. It reminds me without my knowing it of my own hidden anxiety and tends to call it out; hence my irritation. Or again, a man with a great deal of repressed inferiority feeling tends to get annoyed beyond reason with the dominating type of person who reminds him of his own painful feeling of insignificance. Sometimes the mere appearance of such a person will make the old wound begin to throb. In projection we tend to blame another for what is mainly in ourselves. If you look through a dirty window at the sky you may find it hard to tell whether the grey smudge you see is on the window or in the sky. In the same way we see others partly through the window of our own reactions to them; and we tend to read into them qualities which are really in ourselves. The fault I most severely censure in others is a likely pointer to something resembling it in myself.

Everyone has had the experience before an interview of projecting his anxiety or resentment on to the person he was going to see only to find when the meeting takes place that the individual he had feared and resented was in actual fact totally unlike the picture he had painted in advance. The story is told of a motorist stranded on a lonely road at night by a punctured tyre and the want of a jack which would have enabled him to change the wheel. Eventually he decided to walk half a mile across a field towards the light of a farm-house where he hoped to be able to borrow a jack. His mood of irritation and frustration grew stronger and stronger as he approached the house; so that the friendly farmer answering the knock was astonished when he opened the door to be greeted with the words, 'You can keep your damn jack'. The motorist had projected his pent-up anger on to a stranger, very willing to help him, and assumed his request would be refused before he had even made it. It often happens that a person who is angry at getting the worst of an argument accuses his opponent of losing his temper. He is reading his own anger into the other. When a disaster occurs the responsibility for which is very widely distributed, there is a tendency for those implicated to fasten the blame unfairly on one person. The tendency to make scapegoats springs from fear of one's own guilt and the unwillingness to face it. In his *Depth Psychology and a New Ethic*[6] Eric Neumann argues that the Nazis projected their repressed feelings of guilt and inferiority on to the Jews and made them into scapegoats responsible for all Germany's misfortunes. No doubt this scapegoat psychology and the mechanism of projection accounts for much of the bitterness of inter-racial tension today.

No doubt other people (and other races) have undesirable

[6] Hodder and Stoughton 1969 (translated from the original German edition of 1949).

26

qualities and what a man sees in another is unlikely to be wholly projected from himself. The reason why he projects on to one person rather than another is that the person unconsciously selected has certain qualities which make him a more suitable peg on which to hang the projection. It is the strength and irrationality of an antipathy that ought to convince a man that a great deal of what annoys him in another is in fact in himself. A woman was once very badly treated, as she thought, by her sister-in-law. She lay awake at night unable to sleep, arguing her case and proving to her own satisfaction that her sister-in-law had behaved abominably. Round and round in her head went the argument like a noisy merry-go-round making sleep impossible. Suddenly she seemed to hear a still small voice saying to her 'The defendant has admirably stated the case for her own prosecution'. She sat up startled, she thought it out, and then, to her astonishment, realised that the voice was speaking nothing but the truth. It came into her mind that in a different context she had behaved in exactly the way she was blaming in her sister-in-law. With that flash of insight all her resentment went. She had withdrawn her projection, stopped reading her own fault into the other woman and she fell asleep at peace.

Reaction formation and sin

Depth psychology sees this conflict between consciously held aims and ideals and unconscious wishes and fears at variance with them as occurring in all men. The conflict is a triangular one, with the conscious personality at one point of the triangle, endeavouring to come to terms both with the world of people and circumstances around him and the inner world of his largely unconscious fears, desires and impulses. The conflict differs greatly in intensity from one person to another. In one man the tension is crippling, in another so slight that he hardly notices it. Sometimes the conflict is disguised by projection which leads a man to think that he has no inner problems; all his problems are seen as due to the unreasonable and selfish behaviour of other people. Some men are better at responding to the society of their

27

fellow men, others to their own inner world, though, as we have seen, the inner and outer worlds are closely inter-related. Some degree of conflict is universal.

This view of man, as one inwardly at war and hampered in his freedom by the conflict, has much in common with the picture of him that we find in the pages of the New Testament. The New Testament takes it for granted that there is something deeply the matter with man. The trouble has much more to do with sin or sinfulness than with actual sins or misdeeds. He is estranged from God, from his fellows and in his own being. He is a sinner unable to save himself; he is like a lost sheep unable to find his way home; he is like a sick man in need of a doctor; he is in bondage to sin. He is unable to carry out his resolves through some power that frustrates him from within. In his letter to the Romans St Paul describes this inner conflict: 'Instead of doing the good things I want to do, I carry out the sinful things I do not want. When I act against my will, then, it is not my true self doing it, but sin which lives in me' (Rom. 7:19, 20). 'In my inmost self I dearly love God's law, but I can see that my body follows a different law which battles against the law which my reason dictates. This is what makes me a prisoner of that law of sin which lives inside my body' (Rom. 7:22, 23). There are big differences in outlook and temper between St Paul and the modern psychologist. The latter does not make use of the idea of sin, which belongs to the religious context of man's relationship with God. But despite these differences we can discern a strong resemblance. For in the passages just quoted St Paul is describing, in the language of his day, his defeat in his efforts to live in accordance with an ideal by a reaction from the unconscious that nullified these efforts. The terminology is different but the experience of conflict between conscious intention and something within which defeats the intention is the same.

Most people can find parallels in their own experience, though perhaps only in mild forms, with St Paul's inner conflict of duty and desire, of resolve and ability to execute the thing resolved. But St Paul claims to have found a solution of his problems, an end to his frustration. He gained his freedom not by redoubled effort but by faith. Conscious

28

and deliberate effort alone can never overcome the rebellion from the unconscious, for the stronger the attempt to repress it the more violent will be its reaction. He finds deliverance through trust in God, whose character and power has been disclosed for him in Jesus Christ. We have been considering man in the light of depth psychology; we must turn now to consider what light depth psychology can shed on the experience of God and the faith which St Paul writes about. This will be the subject of chapter 2.

2

Depth psychology and the experience of God

In the previous chapter I have sketched some of the characteristics of man as depth psychology understands him. Man's psychic life, his thinking and feeling, form a unity, a whole, of which conscious thinking and deciding is only a small part. The image of the iceberg, part of which is above water and part below, well illustrates this unity but fails to do justice to the dynamism of man and the continual interaction between consciousness and the unconscious. Further, man's conscious ego plays the uniquely important ruling part which distinguishes him from the other animals. His patterns of behaviour are not controlled by instinct in the way that instinct rules animal behaviour. Though man depends on his instincts and can never escape their pressure he can choose goals and pursue ends that are not predetermined by instinct. What gives man this greater command over himself is his much more highly developed consciousness, his greater power of willed attention and his ability to attend to a much wider field of objects and events. This ability of man to concentrate on and pursue a chosen goal makes him less aware of and sensitive to the needs and demands of his own nature. The power to concentrate and the power to repress are part and parcel of the same dominance of the conscious ego.

But if the conscious personality is to rule effectively over the unconscious, it must learn to understand and to reckon with the deep-down urges and impulses from within. Otherwise the unconscious will react in ways that interfere with the plans and decisions of consciousness. The secret of success, or at least of getting the best out of yourself, in many different fields (for example in study, in taking examinations and in sport) lies largely in getting your unconscious to work in harmony with your conscious mind. Every cricketer knows what it is to be in form and to be out of form. When you are at the top of your form, when whatever you attempt comes off better than you expected, when in writing the ideas and words flow easily, it is because your unconscious mind is working along with your conscious effort and intention; at such a time you feel relaxed and confident. On the other hand when everything goes wrong, when you are stale or out of form, when you make simple mistakes and have less energy than usual, it is because for some reason the unconscious is not working with you, it is putting the brakes on, it is working against your conscious intention.

The 'Self' and the experience of God

For the believer God is present as the ruling agent in everything that happens: in the structure of the atom, in the evolution of animal species, in the lives of men, in the interaction of men and women and of groups, classes and nations, and in the history of the human race. He is therefore an invisible and perhaps unknown actor in the life of every person without exception. Religious experience is often thought of as something occasional and as something that some persons have and some do not. But if the believer is right all men stand in a permanent relationship to God whether they know it or not. This is part of what is meant by the doctrine that God is the Creator. Religious experience then can be understood as the conscious realisation of this relationship to God; or, to put the matter another way, as the interpretation of life in the light of this relationship. Some men are more or less continuously aware of God, others have occasional experiences of him whether vivid or weak. But such experiences are in reality just flashes of insight into a relationship that is there all the time. I believe that the depth psychologist whose special study is mental experience can shed light on the experience of God, more especially on the particular experiences that lead men to say 'this is God himself at work'. He can also help those who make no claim to have had any conscious experience of God to identify occasions when they have in fact experienced God without realising it.

Religion and religious experience were the life-long concern of Carl Jung, referred to in the introduction. In a television interview in this country, broadcast not long before his death in 1960 he was asked by the interviewer if he believed in God. 'I don't need to believe in God,' was Jung's reply, 'I know.' Jung claimed to have a vivid awareness of God. He added that it was not for him as a psychologist to pronounce on the question whether this experience was an experience of the God whom Christians and other theists, such as Jews and Moslems, believe in, or whether it was an awareness of the higher dimensions of the human spirit. But he affirmed the experience, however interpreted, to be one of immense importance to men and women.

In his psychological explanation of religious experience Jung makes use of the term, the 'self', borrowed from Indian religion. Depth psychology, as we have seen, regards the human personality as a whole, part of which is conscious and part unconscious. Jung calls this whole, comprising the conscious element and the unconscious, the 'self'. In common with Freud and other depth psychologists he calls the conscious, directing element in the mind the *ego*. Jung points out that the ego is sometimes aware of the pressure and influence on it of the whole personality, that is of the self, that a man may occasionally be aware of a larger self pressing upon the little conscious ego. Many people have an experience of this larger self through music. They are, as they say, taken out of themselves; the ego has its little world, that it understands and directs, broken into by the great world of the whole personality, with its heights and depths, which the music has aroused. Perhaps the experience of being in love is the most usual way that a person is made aware of hitherto unsuspected elements of his total being. T. S. Eliot, the twentieth-century poet of mystical experience, writes of one way in which a person experiences this larger self in what he calls the timeless moment, the moment when time seems to stand still, 'The moment in and out of time'. In an instant of insight a person becomes aware of this whole, of which he, the observing ego, is a part. 'Sudden in a shaft of sunlight';

> the moment in the rose-garden,
> The moment in the arbour where the rain beat,
> The moment in the draughty church at smokefall.[1]

I believe such experiences are all what Jung calls the experience of the self. The experience is often coloured with deep religious feeling, with awe and reverence. Jung often speaks of the conscious mind's experience of the self of which it is a part as though it were an experience of God.

The 'Self' as that through which Man experiences God

We thought in the last chapter of the whole personality as a self-regulating psychic mechanism, like a thermostat. This, taken with Jung's identification of the experience of this whole as an experience of God, gives a clue which can enable the believer to interpret much of his experience in the light of his relationship to God. The same clue can help to give meaning to a great deal of religious language which seems to have lost its relevance. The very word 'God', for example, has become devalued and for many has become altogether meaningless except as an exclamation. It is a result of the secularisation of our culture which has led men to view life and the world without any reference to God. But if there is a connection between the old religious language and the farthest reaches of the personality, then talk about God is highly relevant. Another word that has come to seem meaningless is sin, for the reason that it belongs to the context of man's relationship to God; it is a breach of that relationship. With the devaluation of the idea of God sin inevitably loses its meaning. But if we can understand God as addressing us through the unknown heights and depths of our personalities, then the idea of sin will take on new meaning. It will mean a rebellion against something in oneself; it will involve inner division, with the frustration that is bound to follow from being pulled in two directions at once. Sin as

[1] 'Burnt Norton II' *Four Quartets*, Faber 1944.

disobedience to God may mean nothing, but there are few who have had no experience of inner division and frustration.

The sin of pride

The meaning of sin will stand out more plainly if we consider the sin of pride, which is held to be the chief sin. The word pride is used in different senses, and pride as the typical sin must not be confused with a right self-esteem or a legitimate pride in work (though pride of the sinful kind may easily contaminate a man's proper pride). Pride can be described as a refusal to acknowledge dependence on God or to obey him; it is to make oneself and one's dignity the all-important value in life. If God is addressing a man through his whole personality of which the conscious ego is only a small but very important part, then pride can be understood as the refusal of the ego to acknowledge its dependence on its own depths, the ignoring by the ego of the demands of the unconscious. It is as though a king, or a government, exercised authority in his own interest or that of a small minority regardless of the needs of the nation as a whole. What leads the ego into this attitude is fear. Just as fear of rebellion might put a government on the defensive, so the ego is thrown on the defensive against the desires, the feelings and the impulses of its own nature. The matter is complicated by the ego's triangular relationship, referred to in the last chapter, not only with its own unconscious but with other people. There are two kinds of pride, according as a man feels other people or his own depths to be a greater threat to his ego. Vanity is the kind of pride in which a person relies on the praise or admiration of others to maintain the feeling of his significance. But the truly proud man does not care a fig for the opinions of others; he adheres to the idea of his own importance regardless of protest either from within himself or from outside. There is a defensive quality about the proud person which is bound up with his unwillingness to trust, to be open in his attitude either to the world outside or to the inner world of his total being.

34

The relationship of the ego with the whole personality sheds light further on the meaning of idols and idolatry. It is well known that the Bible condemns the making of images of wood or stone or precious metal to represent God, no doubt because of the false or inadequate ideas of God that such idols would encourage. The worship of idols was a substitute for worshipping the invisible God. To rely on God was felt not to be a wholly adequate protection in danger or difficulty. To rely on an object that you could see, that had actually been shaped by human hands was safer, it was felt, than relying on an unseen God who made severe demands on conduct and whose agents, the prophets, said disturbing things about social justice. But there is not only an idolatry of visible, tangible objects; there is also an idolatry of ideas. A mental idol is a sophisticated substitute for a metal one. Pride always involves the idolatry of an idea of oneself. The proud man, afraid to admit his dependence on his own depths, defends himself against the feeling of insecurity, caused by his would-be independence, by relying on the idea of his own importance. The idea is a dam built against the waters of criticism whether from within himself or from outside. It is an idol on which he relies to maintain his self-esteem. Anything that appears to threaten the idea of his importance will be extremely disturbing to him; an insult is an attack on the idol which helps him to feel secure and will rouse him to wrath and perhaps retaliation. The vain man depends on the praise or the liking of other people to maintain his self-esteem and the failure to obtain these will leave him disturbed and unhappy.

Idolatry can be understood as a means of protecting ourselves against the things we are afraid of. It is a substitute for trusting in God and seems safer; for to trust God genuinely would be to open ourselves to elements within us that we are afraid of and would like to be without. A man who is afraid above everything of his anger makes an idol of himself as mild and unobtrusive in order to keep his aggressiveness at bay. To trust God would seem much too dangerous, for it would involve him in coming to terms with

35

the fact of his anger and aggressiveness, rooted in his God-created nature, and learn to control it and direct it creatively. A man tormented by a deep down feeling of guilt tries to get rid of it by means of the idea of himself as virtuous; he has made an idol on which he relies for his peace of mind instead of on the merciful God present within his guilt feelings. A man who through experiences when he was young is worried by a sense of his insignificance may manage to suppress it by making power his idol, it may be the power that comes from knowledge or wealth or influential position. None of these three sources of power are bad things in themselves but they can very easily be turned into idols which help a man to keep at bay things in himself that he fears. Everything, whether idea, person or institution, that a man relies on to maintain his self-esteem and sense of inner security, instead of relying on God working within the forces that seem to threaten them, takes on something of the character of an idol. An actual image of wood or stone can be understood as a kind of visual aid to help a man concentrate on the idea he relies on to make himself feel secure. Pride understood as the refusal of the ego to acknowledge its dependence on other people and its own depths, and to rely on God acting from both these directions, inevitably leads to idolatry. For the idol is a method of coping with the fears alternative to trusting in God.

The self-inflicted punishment of idolatry

St Paul in the epistle to the Romans from which I have already quoted speaks of vice as God's punishment for idolatry.

> For this reason God has given them up to the vileness of their own desires and the consequent degradation of their bodies, because they have bartered away the true God for a false one, and have offered reverence and worship to created things rather than to the creator. (Rom. 1:24–5)

Psychology can show this penalty as something not imposed from outside but as arising out of the dynamics of man's nature. For we have seen idolatry to have been a means of repression. And if a man represses part of his personality, the repressed element will exercise a distorting influence on his conscious mind; it will interfere with his efforts and intentions. The greater a man's fear of his repressed feelings the more he will rely in self-defence on his idol, whether it be a mental idea, a person, an institution or a cause. The greater the fear the stronger will be the restraint that the repressed feeling will exercise over his thoughts and actions.

The man who has made an idol of power finds it impossible to treat other people as human beings, but only as helps or hindrances to his power. His idolatry of power has isolated him from his fellows; and this isolation (which is part of the definition of hell) is the self-inflicted punishment of pride. The man who has made an idol of his position will become pompous and self-conscious about it, a quality which, though he may be totally unaware of it himself, will form a barrier to natural and friendly relations with others. His idolatry will tend to cut him off him his fellows. In the same way a man who has made an idol of virtue in order to banish the painful feeling of guilt isolates himself. Which of us can endure the 'holier-than-thou' attitude in others? The man who makes an idol of mildness, in order to get rid of his violent temper, is forced to develop a manner which makes it impossible to establish a frank and open relationship with others. There is always an element of exaggeration, of compulsiveness, about an attitude that is determined in part by repressed fears. The ideas designed in one way or another to buttress a man's good opinion of himself against inner misgivings all tend to isolate him. They force him into the position of a king who exercises authority over his kingdom at the cost of making himself friendless and lonely.

But St Paul is thinking less of this effect of repression and idolatry in interfering with a man's conscious and avowed intentions than of the highly destructive effect when the repressed elements break out, when the ego gives up the struggle to control them and allows them to usurp its own ruling function. For there is not only the tyranny of the ego, the conscious directing element in the personality, over the whole; there is also the worse disaster which befalls a man when the ego identifies itself with violent or passionate drives and desires and gives up the task of directing them to specifically human ends. It is as though the violent boisterous and licence-loving elements in a kingdom completely dominate it and hate, lust and debauchery reign. A weak king may be a worse disaster than a tyrant. St Paul in chapter 1 of his Letter to the Romans describes just such a situation, tracing it as we have seen to man's refusal to worship his Creator.

The experience of God's opposition

If my interpretation of repression and idolatry is correct it will follow that a great many people have had an experience of God without knowing it. For those who have felt themselves inhibited in their freedom and prevented from acting as they wished through an inner compulsion which they cannot master or, alternatively, have been driven to go to excess by the same inner compulsion, have had an experience of God. St Paul and a great many Christian thinkers of the past have called it the experience of God's wrath. But the word 'wrath' conjures up in our minds pictures of an angry or cruel man and so cannot be used today without a great deal of explanation. It might be thought of as like the anger of a doctor at the cancer which is killing his patient. But the doctor is not really angry with the cancer, but only determined to destroy it if he can. So we will translate the old idea of God's wrath into the more acceptable one of his unrelenting opposition to everything that is damaging a man. God is opposed to every attempt we make to escape from facing up both to our total being and to the claim on us of others. It would be no solution to our human problems to surrender unconditionally to the demands either of other people or of the unconscious. What is needed is a creative response to the pressures both from outside and from within the personality. Our frustration is due to our unwillingness through fear to respond to God's summons to us to grow to our full stature. No one escapes some frustration due to his drawing back from the demands made on him both by other people and by his own depths. This frustration is an experience of God's oppositon.

38

God's opposition can be seen as the opposition of the whole of what a man is to the tyranny, the obstinacy, the timidity or the weakness of the ego, the guiding element in the personality. The opposition is best understood not in punitive terms as though God were interfering with us from outside but as the coming into operation of certain correctives built into our nature. It can be likened to the automatic switching on of the heat in a thermostatically controlled heating system if you open all the windows on a cold day in January. As the onflow of heat does its best to counteract the effect of the cold air, so the reaction of the unconscious works to correct the misguided actions and attitude of the conscious mind. Repentance is the act by which the ego changes its attitude, like the closing of the windows. It is the ego, the decision-taking part of the personality, that must change, although the personality as a whole is involved in the mistakes. It is the cox who is to blame for steering the boat into the bank though the whole crew shares in the muddle and confusion that result from his bad steering. It was the attempt of the ego to repress a painful experience and its adoption of a life ideal designed to keep it repressed that has led to the inner compulsions and the reaction formations, which have limited its freedom and brought it low.

The remedy for this is to stop being afraid, to stop relying for security on an idea or an object designed to repress what you are afraid of and to put your trust in God, who is present to you in every influence from outside and from within. It often looks as though the advice of the psychologist differs diametrically from that of the religious teacher or guide. For example the psychologist tells a man to accept himself while the religious teacher tells him to deny himself. But the contradiction between the advice of these two counsellors is more apparent than real. For the self we are urged to deny is the ego, the conscious personality, with its false aims, its obsession with security, its timidity; while the self we are to accept includes the unconscious with its great unrealised potential.

Repentance leads to forgiveness. Forgiveness ends the estrangement that the independence, timidity and weakness of the ego has brought about. By the act of confession the ego disowns its independence and admits its egoism; and by so doing helps to break down the mental barriers against the influence of the unconscious. If by opening the windows and letting in the cold air I cause the heat to be switched on, then if I close them the heat will in time be switched off. If the ego renounces its independence the unconscious, whose needs the ego has been flouting, will turn from an enemy into a friend. The admission by the conscious personality of being in the wrong is naturally not so simple as closing windows. For a man acquires habits which cannot be broken in a moment, and therefore acts of confession have to be made and repeated. The reason for this is not to persuade a reluctant God to forgive through sheer persistence, as a child may hope to wear down parental opposition to some cherished project by continually returning to the subject. The purpose of confession is rather to change the attitude of the ego which has got set in a habit of defensiveness against God.

The act by which a man consciously and deliberately disowns his past ways and resolves to change them is often misunderstood through confusing wrong actions and their consequence. What the ego is to blame for is the misguided action which led to some frustrating reaction from the unconscious. But what a man is inclined to blame is not his foolish or wrong action, but the tiresome reaction from within that his action provoked. Let us take the example of a man with a great deal of bottled-up anger which he is only partly aware of. For years he has tried to keep under his anger with the help of a mild propitiating manner. He hardly ever disagrees with anyone and always avoids an argument. He gets anxious when other people quarrel, he goes pale if anyone is angry with him. He is often inwardly angry but is careful never to show it. One day someone takes advantage of his meek and mild manner and provokes him beyond endurance, his self-control breaks down and he loses his temper badly. He is much ashamed of the outburst and blames himself severely for it. He ought rather to blame himself for the meek and mild manner which concealed his real feelings and deceived both himself and other people. The manner made the outburst inevitable, if he were too severely put upon, as well as inviting others to attack him. The explosion of temper could be a salutary warning that there was something wrong with his whole attitude to life. He needed to repent, that is to change.

To take another example, a motorist has an accident due in part to his own careless driving. As a matter of fact he has often driven quite as carelessly as on this occasion. But this is his first accident and he blames himself severely for it, although he has little or no sense of guilt for the fifty other times he has driven carelessly but without having an accident. It is the careless driving that he ought to blame, not the fact that it led to an accident on one occasion. The accident would prove to have a beneficial result if it had the effect of making him drive carefully in future. The mistake is commonly made of lumping both the wrong action and its consequence together and blaming them both indiscriminately. But for practical reasons it is of great importance to put the blame where it belongs, on the ego and not the whole personality, on the cox and not the rest of the crew for the bad steering.

The experience of forgiveness

Because of a deep-seated sense of guilt some people have great difficulty in accepting forgiveness, in believing that they are, or indeed can be, forgiven. Such people, partly consciously, partly unconsciously, reject themselves and feel it right to do so. They must learn to stop doing this if they are to receive forgiveness. They find it difficult to accept themselves, because it seems to them that what they are told to accept is evil and dangerous; and in a sense they are right. But it is their own fear and rejection of elements in themselves that makes those elements dangerous, just as if you chain a dog up and do not allow it enough exercise it is likely to become savage. The believer is apt to see God behind

41

this attitude of self-rejection and suppose that God rejects him because he rejects himself. There is great psychological wisdom in the insistence in the Christian tradition that forgiveness comes through the cross of Christ. For in that man, unjustly sentenced, jeered at, tortured and nailed to a cross, the Christian sees disclosed the character of the God who is active in all that happens. In the crucified man he sees God going the whole way in identifying himself with men and women regardless of their unresponsiveness. If God can go that far in tolerating men as they are, then a man should be able to tolerate himself.

In *The Pilgrim's Progress*, John Bunyan's allegory of the Christian life, there is a vivid description of the experience of forgiveness. Christian, the hero of the story, sets out on his journey to the Celestial City with a burden on his back. He is a man tortured by a sense of guilt and unable to get rid of his burden till he comes, in Bunyan's own words,

> . . . to a place somewhat ascending; and upon that place stood a cross and a little below in the bottom a sepulchre. So I saw in my dream that just as Christian came up with the cross the burden loosed from off his shoulders and fell from off his back; and began to tumble and so continued to do till it came to the mouth of the sepulchre where it fell in and I saw it no more . . . Then was Christian glad . . . he stood still awhile to look and wonder; for it was very surprising to him that the sight of the cross should so ease him from his burden. He looked and looked again until the springs that were in his head began to flow.[2]

In writing of Christian Bunyan describes his own experience. After being tormented for many years by a sense of guilt he learnt through the cross to stop rejecting himself and to enter into the peace of the forgiven, the peace of those who accept themselves because they believe God has accepted them.

People fall into the mistake of supposing they must be good, that they must, at least approximately, live up to their ideal of themselves if they are to be able to accept themselves.

[2] *The Pilgrim's Progress* (World's Classics, OUP) p. 36.

Such an attitude makes genuine self-acceptance impossible. It is the attempt of the ego to make itself acceptable by pushing out of consciousness all elements of its personality that do not seem to square with its ideal. It resembles the belief condemned by St Paul that a person can earn forgiveness by his good works. One of the first steps in the cure of an alcoholic is taken when he accepts the fact that he is an alcoholic. So long as he is unwilling to admit this, but clings to the belief that with an effort he could become a moderate drinker he cannot be cured. He has to accept himself for what he is, a sick man in need of cure. This is equally true of the drug addict. And these extreme cases shed light on the need for every person, if he is to achieve his potential as a human being, to face and accept the bad, the seemingly discreditable side of himself.

The realisation of God's forgiveness, properly understood, enables men to accept themselves; it ends the civil war within the personality. This inward peace, this realisation that they can accept themselves, often follows the realisation that other people accept them. It is natural that this should be so, for the origin of self-rejection is usually in the belief as a child that one is rejected, that one cannot be loved, because one is bad. Many find it impossible to realise God's acceptance of them because of their rejection, as they believe, by their fellows. In Christ's teaching forgiveness always involves other men as well as God. 'Forgive and you shall be forgiven.' 'Forgive us our debts as we forgive those who are indebted to us.' The society Alcoholics Anonymous is probably the most successful of all agencies in helping to rehabilitate alcoholics. One of the key factors in its healing work is the spirit of fellowship, of mutual acceptance that unites its members.

Not only is it true that many cannot accept themselves until they realise that they are accepted by others, it seems also that unless we realise that we are forgiven we cannot forgive. If a man cannot accept himself but is on the defensive against part of his own personality he will find it impossible wholly to accept others. On the other hand if a man has found the peace which comes from having accepted himself he will be able and glad to accept others; he is no longer

43

afraid of the repercussions that such acceptance might have within himself. At peace with God he is at peace within himself and can be at peace with all men.

The experience of God through conscience

We have followed Jung's clue that a man experiences God as he becomes aware of his whole personality influencing his conscious mind; or, to put it differently, God addresses man's conscious mind through the total personality of which it is a part. With the help of this clue we have interpreted God's wrath, that is God's opposition, as the opposition of a man's whole self to the egoism and timidity of his conscious personality. We have applied the same principle to interpret repentance and forgiveness as the change of attitude by the conscious mind which leads to the end of the opposition from unconscious forces within the personality; the result of this change within a person is a peace and harmony within him which makes him open to, and tolerant of, others. Let us go on to use this principle to shed light on the experience a man has of God in the call of duty and the command of conscience.

The first appearance of conscience, as we saw in chapter 1, occurs in the tendency of the small child to identify with parental attitudes and in particular with their approval of certain behaviour as good and other behaviour as bad. Thus the beginnings of conscience and a sense of duty appear to be socially determined. Whatever seed of conscience is implanted in our nature at birth, it requires the influence of society to enable this seed to grow. A person believes he ought to be honest, truthful and considerate because that is what other people think he ought to be. But however much society fosters and shapes it, conscience is more than just the reflection of society's views of right and wrong. Otherwise it would be impossible to explain the fact that the men of supreme ethical insight have mostly been rebels against the standards of the society which educated them. And so long as social considerations dominate a man, so that whatever society thinks to be right he automatically and uncritically agrees to be so, his conscience remains immature. The dictates of this immature, socially dominated conscience are by no means necessarily mistaken; but they are second-hand and sometimes contradict a man's own deepest insights. Sometimes we have to disobey the voice of this immature conscience, reflecting the opinions of society (or perhaps that small unit of society which influences us most profoundly, our family) and put up with the feeling of guilt it may inflict upon us, if we are to obey our true, our mature conscience. True conscience speaks as the voice of the self, of the whole of us, or at least of that element in the whole which most truly represents us. True conscience speaks its mind whatever other people may think or say. When you feel compelled to take some stand against the opinion of most of your contemporaries, when you feel that any other course would be a betrayal, it is because the whole of you has brought influence to bear upon the decision-taking ego, to strengthen it against disinclination and the fear of the consequences of doing right. When a constraining pressure bears upon you from the depths of your being, impelling you to take some action against your apparent interest and the opinion of your friends, you recognise the voice of conscience as the voice of God. God's will may, of course, often be what both inclination and the advice of others point to. But on these occasions we seldom have the sense of doing his will that accompanies actions done in obedience to conscience in the face of public opinion and to our apparent disadvantage.

The imperative of conscience as the voice of God is well illustrated by some of the Hebrew prophets. Amos, for example, felt compelled to leave his countryman's occupation to go to the court of the king of Israel and denounce the idolatry of the nation and its accompanying social injustice – the exploitation of the poor by the rich by means of trickery or violence. When rebuked and told to stop prophesying or do it somewhere else he replied in effect: 'I am no prophet, I'm just an ordinary man, a small farmer, but the Lord said to me "Go and speak out plainly to my people" ' (see Amos 7:12–15). 'The lion has roared; who is not afraid? The Lord God has spoken; who can refuse to declare his message?' (Amos 3:8). We meet the same accents in Martin Luther's 'Here I stand, I can do no other'. What gives a man the

45

strength to take this stand in the face of all opposition is the support of his own unconscious depths and heights, which mobilise all his strength and fighting energy to stand firm. It is not easy to say with certainty when the authentic voice of conscience is speaking. A man's conscience may be in error, whether from ignorance of facts bearing on the decision he believes he must make or from a mistaken assessment of them. But despite this possibility Christian moralists insist that when conscience speaks clearly it must always be obeyed. For this reason a civilised state allows the right of an individual on grounds of conscience to refuse to fight in a war. This principle is not overthrown should the state impose certain penalties upon the conscientious objector, in order to discourage men from irresponsibly opting out of an unpleasant and dangerous task.

The experience of divine guidance

My next two illustrations of the experience of God will be taken from the ordinary practice of prayer, the practice of asking God for guidance in perplexity and for help in trouble. A man seeking to discover God's will when having to take a decision in some perplexing situation will begin, probably, by thinking the matter out as thoroughly as he can. He will weigh up the pros and cons of the possible courses of action and will very likely take advice. Having done this he will pray for guidance by first acknowledging his blindness, ignorance and lack of insight and then beg God to make known his will. It is the blindness and ignorance of the ego, the directing element in the personality, that he is especially acknowledging. And he prays to God believing that he will address him through his own depths (though the unsophisticated believer will not think in these terms). Prayer for guidance made in this way constantly leads to fresh insight. Sometimes a person may be confirmed in what he had already come to think was the best course; sometimes a course which had not seemed a good one takes on a different appearance and he sees it as the one he must follow; sometimes some new and relevant fact will come to mind which sheds fresh light on the matter to be decided.

The act by which a man admits the incapacity of conscious and deliberate reflection to solve his problems throws the conscious mind open to the wisdom and experience of the whole personality. This buried experience begins to become available to a man as in the act of trusting God he opens himself to the wisdom of the unconscious. Of course the deliverances of the unconscious are by no means infallible. They need to be scrutinised and tested as far as they can by the conscious ego that has to take the decisions. But God guides men through the whole of what they are, the unconscious as well as the conscious; and it is in his guidance through the unconscious, with its unexpected suggestions and inspired guesses, that we most easily come to realise that it is God who is guiding us; just as we most easily discern his voice in conscience when it tells us to act against the commonly accepted moral standard. The dream, as was noted in chapter 1, is one of the ways that the unconscious speaks to the conscious mind. The dream was reckoned in ancient times (for example in the Bible and the Koran) to be one of the ways that God guided men. St Peter's dream at Joppa, mentioned in chapter 1, is a single instance out of a great many in the Bible of God guiding someone through a dream.

God: the strength of those in trouble

Those who believe in God turn to him in time of trouble. Guidance is one type of the help that he gives to those who seek it from him. To rely fully on God is to trust him as acting through the whole of one's personality, not only in the people and events that affect one's life from outside. As the king in a crisis seeks to enlist the whole of his country to help him, so the ego needs to bring the unconscious into action behind it. Immense reserves of energy and initiative which cannot ordinarily be tapped are stored within us. In moments of crisis these inner resources often become available. A mother whose child's life is in danger will keep going day and night nursing the child with hardly any rest, so long as the crisis lasts. Some people are known to be at their best in a crisis, which means that the spur of danger or opportunity enables them to draw on these latent reserves. Many have had the experience when under extreme pressure of the strain increasing almost to breaking point. Then at the very moment when they felt they must collapse under the strain there has followed the experience of being apparently taken over by a power greater than themselves and they have found themselves acting with a force and decisiveness quite outside their usual range. The whole self has come to the support of the struggling ego just as a whole people might unite in support of their king when their country was under threat of invasion.

St Paul, writing out of experience, affirms that God's strength is made perfect through human weakness; that when he is weak he is strong with the strength of God (see 2 Cor. 12:9, 10). Only when ego feels itself weak and defenceless is it prepared to throw down its defences against the influences of the unconscious and open itself to the reinforcing energy from within. The needle of crisis and faith in God together enable a man to face the risk of opening himself to the unknown energies within him. This is perhaps the commonest of all experiences of God. It is summed up in the Psalm verse: 'When I was in trouble I called upon the Lord: and he heard me.' Those who in a crisis, sincerely and with real faith in the God who rules throughout their whole being, beg his help, do find themselves inwardly renewed. Urgent prayer brings swift help.

To illustrate this principle; a student gets stuck in writing an essay. His grasp of his subject is confused. He tries to set down his ideas but the words will not come; he tries to analyse the subject but his divisions overlap or are artificial, not springing from the subject matter itself but imposed by him across the grain. At last he gives up in despair; he drops the essay, reads, turns on the radio or goes for a walk. Later, perhaps the next day, he returns to his essay and finds everything has changed. The pieces of the jig-saw that had seemed unrelated fit together; the subject becomes clear; he is able to analyse it convincingly and write fluently. By dropping work on the essay he allowed the unconscious to complete the work for him. He trusted his unconscious and his unconscious did not let him down. It may be thought that to draw this parallel between the way a man's mind works when writing an essay and prayer to God for help is to undermine faith in the value of prayer. But this is by no means so. It was pointed out in the introduction that the fact that autosuggestion is at work in prayer in no way disproves the validity of prayer. So, the uncovering of certain psychological mechanisms at work in prayer for help, in no way disproves the belief that God answers prayer; for God, if there is a God, is the author of the mechanisms. On the contrary it merely shows that the practice of asking help from God in time of difficulty is highly relevant to the business of living and working effectively.

The experience of God's presence

My final example of the experience of God is less common than the previous examples and more difficult to describe: the experience of God's presence within one's own personality. One of the aims of the old spiritual guides was to train and focus the awareness of God's indwelling presence. According to Jung's theory men experience God as the experience of their whole self. These guides seem to locate the experience of God in various regions of the personality. But their words must be understood as metaphors hinting at a vivid experience baffling simple description. They speak of the base of the soul as the place of the divine encounter, indicating the experience to be the most fundamental that a man can have, like the experience of the ground on which he stands. They speak of God as to be found in the apex of the soul, its topmost point, suggesting that the experience of God is the most sublime of human experiences. They allude to the divine spark, suggesting that the experience of God is like that of a leaping flame within, which points to the dynamic, life-enhancing quality of the experience. But perhaps the most significant of all the metaphors is that of the soul's centre as the focus of the divine presence and action.

The metaphor of the centre is closely related to that of the self, of the whole personality. A centre implies a circle or an area of which it is the centre. The centre of a circle is equidistant from every point on its circumference and to say that God acts on the conscious personality through the centre in no way contradicts the statement that he acts upon it through the self. Jung has affirmed that his patients sometimes dreamt of this larger self that enclosed the little ego under the symbol of a mandala, an Eastern symbol in the shape of a square or circle, sometimes intricately patterned, having a centre. A mandala was a symbol devised as a focus of concentration and represents balance, harmony and completeness. The metaphor of the centre suggests that the experience of God within is an experience of being integrated, centred, made one. Some psychologists make use of the idea of the personality centre, a point of balance within the personality. But we are here considering not God's action but man's experience of it; and only those who have attained a certain maturity realise God as acting from a centre within them.

Man's grandeur and wretchedness, his longing for life in depth and his sense of life's triviality, his desire for communion with a reality greater than himself and his sense of exclusion from it, is a very old theme. It is present as an undercurrent of pathos and nostalgia in much pop music. Occasionally this yearning for something greater than the ego can grasp is plain for all to see. George Harrison, one of the Beatles, in his song, *Within you and without you*, sings of 'the space between us all and the people who hide behind a wall of illusion', 'of the people who gain the world and lose their soul'; and 'Try to realise it's all within yourself, no one else can make you change. And to see you're only very small and life flows on within you and without you.' The little ego, out of touch with the self, is out of touch with other people, it hides behind its illusions and idolatries and so shuts itself away from life, from the centre, from God.

A man's personality contains opposite tendencies that pull him first one way then another. There is the urge to dominate and the urge to submit, to turn outwards to others and to retire into his shell, to dance for joy and to throw himself down in despair, to aspire to spiritual things and to respond to the strong pull of the flesh. Through this pendulum swing, this alternation from one pole to its opposite, the conscious personality experiences the self and behind the self perhaps without an inkling of the fact he experiences God. As through faith he comes to be less afraid of this ebb and flow and more open to its influence he may become increasingly aware of a centre within himself. This centre then begins to hold the contrary tendencies in a creative tension and with his co-operation to harness them in the service of the personality as a whole. The centre becomes both a point of focus through which a man can direct his attention to God and also the point through which he can respond to God's guidance over his life. Many spiritual guides call this centre the heart, which should be understood neither as the physical organ that keeps the blood circulating nor as a metaphor for the emotions or even for love, but as the centre where man can find God.

Self-knowledge and the knowledge of God

The old spiritual guides teach men the way to find God within. The first step according to a great many of them is to gain self-knowledge and especially the knowledge of the discreditable side of one's character; that is, in the language of depth psychology, to uncover the feelings and desires which have been repressed because they damage the self-esteem of the ego. Here are words from the fourteenth-century treatise on contemplative prayer called *The Cloud of Unknowing*: 'Therefore swink and sweat in all that thou can'st and mayest for to get thee a true knowing and feeling of thyself as thou art. And then, I trow, soon after that thou wilt get thee a true knowing and feeling of God, as he is.'[3] Despite their quaint, archaic ring the words have a curiously modern sound. The way to the knowledge of God runs through self-awareness. God addresses a man through the self, through the whole of what he is, and ignorance of himself blinds him to the knowledge of God. The title 'Cloud of Unknowing' suggests something of the intuitive nature of this knowledge of God within. The man who knows in this way is standing at the boundary of his understanding's

[3] *The Cloud of Unknowing*, ch. 14.

grasp, he is at the land's edge facing the illimitable ocean. He looks towards God, the Unknown, the mystery which his understanding cannot contain, and the verbal tools by which he labels and dissects the world around him are well-nigh useless.

I have tried to describe the awareness of God's presence within. It is because we are dimly aware of God's presence in ourselves that we recognise his presence outside, in the world of nature for instance. There is the well-known incident of the eighteen-year-old French boy, Nicholas Herman, who later entered a monastery and became known as Brother Lawrence, the author of the book, *The Practice of the Presence of God*. He was staring one winter day at a tree stripped of its leaves. Presently he reflected that in a few weeks' time the tree would put forth bud, leaf, blossom and finally fruit, and further that God's providence brought this yearly miracle about. On the instant his heart went out in love and trust to God, and there came upon him an awareness of God that never left him through a long life. Examples of this kind could be multiplied. Why was it that the sight of that tree made so lasting an impression on that teenager? I think it sparked off something that was waiting to be set on fire. It brought into the full light of consciousness an awareness of God within that was pressing for recognition.

In this chapter we have been using the experience of the self as a clue to man's experience of God. I have tried to show how through the pressure of the whole personality God judges and opposes the ego, the decision-taking element in it and leads it to change; how through the total personality God commands the ego and confronts it with duty; how he guides and helps a man through the man's own inner resources; how he makes his presence known to a person through his own inner being. In trying to make a complex subject intelligible, I have greatly oversimplified the account and have left many gaps, and in particular have failed to bring out two important points. First I have too much treated the individual as if he were in isolation from his fellows, which is to falsify the facts of our situation. Men only realise their humanity through interaction with other men. God addresses us through the personalities of other people as well as through our own depths. The second omission is that though much has been said about the experience of God there has been little about faith. The writers of the New Testament and those for whom they wrote had had a profound experience of God mediated to them through Jesus Christ. But they write not about the experience of God but about faith in him. Faith is by no means identical with experience though a mature faith in God includes some experience of him. In the next chapter something must be said to make good these two omissions.

3

Belief and growth to maturity

In the previous chapter use was made of Jung's concept of the self, that is the total personality, to illuminate man's experience of God. If we believe in God we shall believe that he is acting on us in a million ways of which we are as wholly unconscious as we are of the earth travelling round the sun at the speed of some sixty thousand miles an hour. But I believe that it is through his total personality of which the conscious, decision-taking ego is but a part that a person normally becomes aware of, experiences, God's action. There are those who accept the validity and importance of this experience without accepting the theistic explanation of it. This book, as I have said, makes no attempt to prove the existence of God but only its practical relevance supposing it is true.

Experience and faith

Jung claimed to have an intuitive knowledge or experience of God. I have already quoted his reply to the question 'Do you believe in God?' 'I don't need to believe, I know.' Jung has defined belief as perception through the unconscious. When a person has an intuition he knows without being able to say how he knows; he has a hunch, something tells him, he jumps at the solution of a problem without having consciously worked the sum out. Intuition, though by no means infallible and requiring to be checked and verified if there is any means of doing so, surprisingly often proves to be correct. Many scientific advances have been made through intuition leaping over difficulties and guessing the solution of some vexing problem. Often it has taken much patient experiment to demonstrate the truth of what was seen in a

moment of insight. There is the well-known c
German chemist Kekulé, who when investigatin
ture of benzene, a compound of carbon and hydrog
a dream which led him to postulate its ring structure. It too.
many months of experiment to confirm what is now the
generally accepted hypothesis. An even better known
example from the ancient world is that of Archimedes, who,
puzzling over the problem of discovering whether a royal
crown was made of pure gold or had had base metal alloyed
with it by its manufacturer, hit on what is now called the
principle of specific gravity, when in a bath he noticed the
displacement of water by his body. The principle seized in a
moment of intuition has since been confirmed by innumerable experiments.

This intuitive experience of God, however, is not the
precise equivalent of faith in him, for, though a full faith
includes an experience of God, it goes further. Faith always
involves venture; it means accepting the intuition of God as
genuine and putting it to the test of practical action. Abraham
is given in the Bible as the typical man of faith, not because
he had many experiences of God, but because he took his
experience seriously, because he made the venture of faith
in obedience to it, leaving his ancestral home in Mesopotamia
and setting out across the desert to a destination unknown.
Nicholas Herman, mentioned in the last chapter, expressed
his faith by entering a monastery. Albert Schweitzer, with
an international reputation both as theologian and musician,
expressed his faith by abandoning two possible careers in
order to train as a doctor and found a hospital at Lambaréné
in the Congo. As a scientific hypothesis needs to be tested
by experiment, so the experience of faith has to be tested
by its translation into action. The God who addresses the
conscious personality of every man through the whole of
what he is, addresses him also through the world around
him, through the needs and demands of other people,
through the happenings that affect him. Faith in God orients
a person not only to his own depths but to other people and
to all the problems of living. God is not only my personal
centre; he is also 'the still point of the turning world'.

Faith is a means to deeper understanding and fuller life.

St Augustine, the fifth-century bishop of Hippo in North Africa, pointed out the importance of faith for understanding in his saying: 'I believe in order to understand.' Faith like some sound scientific hypothesis, convinces partly by its power to explain what was dark. It makes sense of man's deepest experience. But faith is also a means to fuller life because it encourages him to take the risks that a full life demands. Safety first is a sound principle in certain dangerous situations: down a coal mine, when taking off or landing in an aeroplane, or when chopping steps on a glacier with an ice axe on a mountain climb. But safety first as a life principle narrows and deadens. Faith fosters a fuller life because it is a principle of venture. 'Fear not, only believe,' said Christ to his disciples. And 'Why are ye so fearful, O ye of little faith?' A full, mature life demands courage and if faith helps a person to face life unafraid it is certainly highly relevant to the achievement of maturity. This will become clearer when we examine more closely what maturity means.

Maturity

Maturity is an elusive quality when we use it of man. We say that a full grown dog or cat is a mature animal but when we apply the term to man we mean more than a physically adult human being. In *The Integrity of the Personality*[1] the psychiatrist, Anthony Storr, defines maturity as self-realisation, which he explains as the fullest possible expression in life of the potentialities of the individual, the realisation of his own uniqueness as a personality. He adds to this rough definition as a further working hypothesis, that every man consciously or unconsciously seeks this goal of self-realisation or maturity.[2] If we accept the definition of maturity as self-realisation it is clear that maturity is never completely achieved, though some approximate more closely to it than others. Further, dynamic psychology insists that emotional maturity is characterised by the ability to become interested in things and persons. In other words a capacity for altruism

[1] Penguin 1970.
[2] Ibid., p. 27.

56

is one fundamental characteristic of emotional maturity. In fact the more a person realises and accepts himself, the more he is able to accept other people.

It follows from this that genuine self-realisation is in no way a selfish goal. It cannot be attained without others or at their expense. To quote Storr again:

> . . . the development of the individual and the maturity of his personal relationships proceed hand in hand and one cannot take place without the other. Self-realisation is not a selfish principle; it is firmly based on the principle that men need each other in order to be themselves, and that those people who succeed in achieving the greatest degree of independence and maturity are also those who have the most satisfactory relations with others.[3]

The truth of our mutual interdependence can be illustrated from the mental illness called schizophrenia, in which the sufferer is almost completely withdrawn into a private inner world of his own. He interprets all that is said to him or done for him in terms of his own inner world. For example, he may be convinced that other people are in a conspiracy to do him some injury, and whatever anyone says is twisted so as to fit in with this inner conviction. He does not *hear* what people say or see them as existing in their own right; they are just participants in a drama that is being enacted in his own mind. This isolation from other people tends to destroy the patient's individuality. There are many different kinds of schizophrenia. But those who have had the care of schizophrenics in a mental hospital comment on their similarity. The individual quirks, the unexpected points of view, that you come across in any casual group of people seem to get ironed out in schizophrenia, which isolates a man from his fellows. It is contact with people that draws out a man's individuality. The most complete individual is the man satisfactorily related to his fellows.

[3] Ibid., p. 32.

Mature and immature relationships

Let us try to focus the idea of maturity more sharply by considering the attitude of the mature to other people. Jung described this attitude as unprejudiced objectivity. The mature man does not pass judgements on a person either in thought or word. This does not mean that he is indifferent to right or wrong, to cruelty, greed or dishonesty. But in his relationships he has a deep respect for people as they are, for facts and events and for the person who suffers them.[4] There are two opposite ways of failing to treat maturely someone who has acted, let us say, in a most selfish and callous way. One would be expressed in the words, spoken or merely thought, 'I have nothing but contempt for a man who can behave like that.' The other could be expressed by 'I wouldn't presume to have any opinion of my own about the man's conduct.' In a mature relationship a man neither condemns another nor abandons his own standards. He, as he is, confronts the other, as he is. One man or woman faces another with interest but without fear and without concealment. This is an ideal to which most people can only hope to approximate and then perhaps only with two or three individuals, it may be only with one.

Two other immature attitudes are those of domination and submission, both of which are referred to in the saying: 'If you can't lick them, join them.' Both make a mature relationship impossible. If I can only feel at home with others when I am thrusting my views on them and getting them to agree, then I am not respecting them at all. I am treating them as a means to bolstering up my insecure ego. But to adopt the opposite attitude, always agreeing with others and never expressing disagreement, whatever my real opinions are, is equally immature and equally makes any mature relationship impossible. For such a relationship implies the ability of a person to stand up for himself and affirm what he really thinks and feels. This is not to be confused with the self-assertiveness which is the ego's defence against its insecurity. Mature self-affirmation springs from a sense of inner security rooted in self-acceptance.

[4] C. G. Jung, *Modern Man in Search of a Soul* (Kegan Paul 1936), p. 270).

The essential immaturity of the relationships based on domination or submission is in no way lessened when it is coloured by affection. In this case the attitude is seen clearly for what it is as the extension into adult relationships of what was appropriate enough as between parent and child, but has become out of place. Erich Fromm[5] described four common types of immature character. They are four strategies which the ego, afraid to accept itself, adopts in order to defend itself in its consequent weakness. As no one achieves complete maturity everyone can probably discover traces of himself in one or other of the types. The first is the receptive character who believes that everything he wants comes from outside himself. He depends on others for knowledge, security and love. He does not hesitate to show himself as helpless and incompetent, for this will appeal to the protective instinct in others. He is glad to be taken care of and when he feels secure is happy, genial and affectionate. He relies on others for reassurance in the face of his sense of insecurity.

A second immature type is called by Fromm the exploitative character. He is the exact opposite of the receptive character. He is aggressive, he would rather get his way by force or cunning than by relying on the co-operation of others. He is apt to be negative and destructive in his attitude to others and unwilling to co-operate, except on his own terms. If I am of this type I shall tend to be critical of others. The more I criticise, the more I demonstrate my superiority to those I criticise. By running down the authorities of the college or institution I belong to I absolve myself from the responsibility of working to make it better. By declaring that politics is a dirty game and all politicians have a personal axe to grind I thereby defend my own political irresponsibility. My destructive attitude to others betrays my defensiveness, my immaturity.

A third type of person is called by Fromm a hoarding character. He is interested in his own possessions, his own discoveries, but not in those of others. He shows his defens-

[5] See J. A. C. Brown, *Freud and the Post-Freudians* (Pelican 1969), ch. 8, especially pp. 161–2.

iveness by opting out of life's excitements and extravagances, so far as he can. He is usually neat and orderly in his habits. He never attempts anything that is not well within his power. He lives in a small world. He avoids risks and if against his will he is involved in some adventure outside his control he will be very ready to cut his losses and run for safety.

A fourth type of person, called by Fromm the marketing character is equally defensive. He is chameleon-like in his ability to adapt himself to the opinions and values of whatever society he finds himself in. He cannot bear to be isolated. He is so anxious to please others that he resembles a salesman anxious to persuade others to accept not the Encyclopaedia Britannica, nor the latest detergent, but himself. At bottom he is seeking to be reassured as to his value by other people's acceptance of him.

Fromm describes a fifth type of person, the mature man, as the productive character, because he is able to love others disinterestedly, for themselves, and not just to satisfy a need of his own. But no one is fully mature, and maturity and immaturity are relative concepts. Maturity is relative in another way. There is a maturity proper to age. We should not call a child of eight immature who behaved in the way children usually do at that age, but we should say this of a boy or girl of fourteen who behaved like an eight-year-old. We should call a man of forty who behaved like an undergraduate immature but not a man of twenty who behaved in the same way. Again, a man may be mature in some respects and not in others. A man of mature intelligence may be emotionally immature, while many men and women who are extremely naïve in their thinking about science or politics strike us as fully mature persons. Further, a person's career or occupation may affect the way we judge his maturity. We don't expect the same kind of maturity in an explorer as in a university professor, in a farmer or an engineer as in a professional writer. But making allowance for the variables due to age, circumstance or calling we can say that a man can only become mature in relationship with others and that the mature relationship is one of deep and sensitive respect for the reality of the other, which is only possible for those who have learnt to accept and affirm themselves.

Maturity might be described in a phrase of Fairbairn as 'mature dependence'. A man is inescapably dependent on other men, as a castaway on a desert island would quickly realise, particularly if he had no books written by other men or desert island discs to mitigate his loneliness. The mature, while accepting this dependence as fundamental, have yet attained a certain independence. Like the canoeist who is free and at home on the river which bears his canoe, so the mature man feels himself free and at home in the society of his fellows. He can take the lead when occasion demands without self-consciousness or follow the leadership of others without any servility because he accepts himself; and his peace of mind does not depend either on dominating or being ruled by others. But this maturity can only be won by facing and overcoming fear.

The development of maturity

All this becomes more apparent when we turn from the mature dependence of the adult to the total dependence of infancy and trace the gradual growth to maturity. We thought earlier of the relationship of the conscious personality to the unconscious as resembling that of a king to the country over which he rules. To begin with, the ego is by no means an independent ruler. The child's personality is much more like a colony ruled over by parents than an independent state. The conscious personality of the child develops slowly and only step by step does the ego grow strong enough to become independent and free from the need of external control.

The need of a strong and mature ego may appear to conflict with what was said earlier about egoism and the need for the ego to change its attitude. But actually it is the weak ego that tends to be egoistic and unable to respond creatively either to other people or to its own depths. Sometimes its weakness expresses itself in a repressive attitude to the unconscious and one of stiffness to other people, as a weak man sometimes becomes a stickler for discipline.

The foundation of a strong and mature ego is laid in the home and especially during the first five years of life. As we have seen, our ability to cope with the world around us depends largely on our ability to cope with the world within, and especially with the painful feelings we would like to be rid of. Nothing is a greater help to this self-acceptance than the assurance that we are accepted by others. Accordingly in addition to their need of food and warmth and a great deal of physical care and attention babies have one great emotional need, the need of love. C. J. Adcock illustrates this need from a study of ten institutions for the care of unwanted babies, made fifty years ago in the U.S.A. when the needs of babies were not understood as they are today. In nine out of ten of the institutions that were studied not one of the babies who entered the institution under the age of one survived to the age of two. Their physical needs were adequately attended to, they died because they lacked the love that a mother normally delights to give her baby.[6]

This essential love is of two kinds. First and foremost there is the need of the unconditional, all-accepting love of a mother for her child, the love that envelops and protects him, however trying and bad-tempered, however much of a nuisance he may be. Sometimes, the child experts say, a child is deliberately naughty, unconsciously prompted to it in order to satisfy a doubt, to make quite certain that mother loves him despite the worst that he can do. Sometimes a child steals because he craves affection; the money he takes is a substitute for the love which is what he really wants. The mother is the major part of the infant's world; if the child is convinced from his own experience that his mother delights in him he will begin life with the sense that the world is a happy, welcoming place. Perhaps nothing is so important for a child's later growth to maturity as the certainty of his mother's unconditional love.

But once this certainty has been sufficiently established another kind of love becomes important, the conditional love that makes demands, that disapproves of the child when he behaves badly, that insists that he be good. For in addition to the basic assurance of unconditional love, the deep certainty that he is loved for himself without any strings

[6] C. J. Adcock, *Fundamentals of Psychology* (Penguin 1970), pp. 53–4.

attached, the child also needs the assurance that his bad impulses and behaviour, which he secretly fears but cannot control, will not be permitted but will be checked and corrected. The child values some external discipline when he knows that there is love behind it. There is another reason why the love that makes demands is important. The unconditional love of mother is a gift that comes from outside; it is of grace; either he has it or he has not; there is nothing that he can do about it. But the love that makes demands can be won. The small child knows that mum or dad will be pleased with him if he does what they expect. He has an incentive to effort, to good behaviour, to grow out of childish ways.

It is usual to associate the first of these kinds of loving with mother and the second with father, though in actual practice both mother and father may love in either or both of these ways. The difference between these two kinds of love may reside more in the mind of the child than in the feelings of the parents. Life is simpler for the child if he can associate comfort and consolation with mother and discipline and authority with father. He knows where he stands and what to expect; and wise parents realise this and co-operate in their child's interest. The assurance that he is circled and sustained by the strong love of father and mother enables a child to accept himself, to cope with his feelings of rage and fear without undue repression, and to grow up with an open and trusting disposition that it will take a great deal to destroy.[7]

Obstacles to the development of maturity

Both these kinds of love are needed if a child is to grow up with a strong and mature ego. A child who failed to receive one of them may be obsessed all his life with what as a child he lacked. He will be driven in search of a mother substitute or a father substitute to satisfy a need that his actual father or mother failed to meet. The growing child passes through

[7] See Erich Fromm, *Art of Loving* (Allen and Unwin, paperback edition), pp. 33–8; also for a fuller treatment, D. W. Winnicott, *The Child, the Family and the Outside World*, Penguin 1969.

a number of stages each with its own special needs. If the needs of each stage are sufficiently met, then the child goes on contentedly to the next stage. But if it is not met at the right time the child's development is partly held up; he harks back to the past, hankering after what he never had at the time he needed it. The child who never had the sense of being loved unconditionally will have a craving for this kind of love which he will find it hard to satisfy. He will tend to feel unsure of himself and will continually need to be reassured. He will unintentionally destroy a friendship through the excessive demands he makes on his friend. He will try to get from his friend the attention and care that it is reasonable for a child to expect from his mother but not for one adult to expect from another. Equally the boy who lacked kindly but firm discipline when he needed it may develop a craving for some external authority over him which he may satisfy by joining the army, by embracing some authoritarian political system or in some other way. He is trying to make good a deficiency in his upbringing.

These are not the only ways in which children may fail to get what they need. Sometimes a father may be too authoritarian (or too authoritarian for the rather sensitive child) with the result that the child grows up a rebel against all authority, however reasonable. He was not allowed sufficient independence as a child and so he develops an exaggerated need to be independent, he becomes the so-called natural rebel. Again, a mother's love may be affectionate to the point of smothering her child with more affection than he wants. This will tend to threaten his independence just as much as the sternness of a too authoritarian father. Later he will very likely rebel not against authority but against affection, and will find it very difficult to enter into warm and intimate relations with anyone.

In sum a child has a fundamental need to be treated with a love that shows deep respect for him as a person. But the only parents capable of meeting this need adequately are those who have themselves reached some degree of emotional maturity. A mother who has repressed her aggression and has never come to terms with it is likely to be deeply disturbed by her child's reaction of rage and hate when frustrated, as he is bound to be sometimes by not being allowed to have what he wants. She will feel her child's rage as a threat to herself; her own repressed anger will be awakened and she will feel insecure. She will feel a sudden uprush of rage against her baby who is being so tiresome; and the baby, sensing this reaction in his mother, will feel it is unsafe to be angry with mother and will do his best to repress his rage and comply with his mother's demands. Again, every child passes through a phase when he is intensely interested in his excretory functions. Some mothers feel somewhat shocked by this and perhaps unwittingly cause their child to feel there is something unclean about these functions and to repress their interest. Some children feel that they must repress a good deal of what they really like if they are to be what their parents consider nice children.

Only mature parents can avoid reacting to their children in ways that may do them harm. They must be neither over-dominant nor over-compliant; they must neither force their children to conform to their ideas nor yet be afraid to affirm what they do really think and feel. A boy or girl has not only a right to have his own personal opinions respected but the right also to know what his father and mother really think and feel. Often a boy or girl will not ask advice from his parents, not because their opinions are despised but because there are apt to be too many emotional strings attached to parental advice. They fear that their parents would be shocked if they knew some of the things they thought and wanted. They fear too that their parents will be hurt or angry if they reject advice given; and some parents justify the fear. But if children are to grow up there must be some rebellion against parental attitudes. No boy or girl can be content to be the pale shadow of father or mother. Mature parents understand this and do not feel hurt, threatened or let down when their children choose a different road from their own.

The transition from child to boy or girl to man and woman is difficult. The young child needs a great deal of protective love. As he grows older he needs less of the love that protects and more of the love that trusts him to learn and grow through his own experience. It is difficult for parents, however wise, to change their attitudes so as to keep perfect pace with the changing needs of their children. It is not surprising that parents have a difficulty in understanding their teenage sons and daughters and vice versa. Further, a boy or girl is often torn by an inner struggle which he does not understand between the old need to be dependent and the new need for freedom. He is apt to blame his parents for the feeling of childish dependence which they cannot help awakening and which he resents. Mature parents realise what a difficult and delicate matter it is to give sufficient support to their children through all the stages of their growing up without damaging their proper independence.

Maturity and the ego ideal

A person's experience in later life is always deeply coloured by the way he experienced life in his earliest and most formative years. It takes most people a long time to grow out of all childish attitudes if they ever do. There is a tendency under stress to hark back to the attitudes and ways of coping with life that were developed early. The commonest instance of this is in severe illness when the sick person frequently reverts to habits of obedience or naughtiness which he acquired as a child. A secure home background is the greatest help in fostering the growth of a strong and secure ego. The background, however, is never perfect. For one thing children differ greatly and the background that is right for one child may be quite wrong for another of different temperament.

One of the ways in which we grow out of dependence on parents is through the development of an ego ideal, that is an ideal of the kind of person one wants to become. To begin with, the child partly consciously models himself on his parents; a boy wants to be like father, a girl like mother. Later on, loved and respected relatives, friends and teachers modify the ideal. Boys and girls tend to make heroes whom they unconsciously and sometimes deliberately imitate. This is a perfectly normal and natural phase to pass through. One's hero gives one the incentive to put away childish things and grow up, to attempt difficult and demanding feats, to exercise the self-discipline necessary if one is to

66

become like one's hero. It is of the greatest importance that an ego ideal should be realistic, that is based on real talent and aptitutde. It will not be helpful for an unathletic boy to aim at becoming a star footballer nor a girl without good looks or acting ability to hope to succeed as an actress. It is possible to have an ego ideal so unrealistic that it is bound to hinder growth to maturity till it has been abandoned. An impossible ideal will drive a person to despair because of his inability to approach anywhere near it.

An ego ideal can easily be distorted into a means by which a person represses elements in his personality that he should accept. A boy may be afraid of his natural aggressiveness because of the trouble it has caused him in the past; and instead of learning to accept and control it he seeks to be rid of it altogether. This may lead him to choose for his ideal humility misinterpreted as the negation of all aggressiveness and the attempt to become as much like a doormat as possible. Or again a boy or a girl may have developed a fear of sex and especially of its physical side; this may lead him to form an ideal of purity mistakenly thought of as meaning the negation of sex which if it is strongly held will tend to repress sex feeling and push it right out of control. Genuine purity involves not the denial of sex but its control. Fear of sex distorts the true ideal of purity into something damaging to the growth of the person who holds to it. These ideals, which, rightly understood, would have helped the growth of a mature personality, have been distorted by fear into a hindrance to it.

Faith and growth to maturity

In the arduous achievement of maturity a genuine faith in God is an immense help. For genuine faith implies an attitude of venture, of risktaking, of facing and surmounting obstacles. Intellectual insight alone into the groundlessness of the fears that prevent him from acting creatively will not get rid of the fears. He must take the risk of acting despite his misgivings if he is to overcome them. The patient is never cured in the analyst's consulting room. He gets well as he learns to use the insights he has gained there to face his problems and live his life more creatively. Genuine faith in God helps a man to face the various fears that may unman him. A painful experience of the past may lead a man to evade every situation that might lead to its repetition. A person can become so discouraged by repeated failure that he dreads and avoids any task that might possibly be beyond his strength. One who has suffered from having been severely and perhaps undeservedly blamed may come to dread doing anything that might incur criticism. A boy or girl thrust into premature responsibility may develop a fear of responsibility that leads him to evade plain duties. All these fears if not overcome will prevent a person's growth to maturity.

Some persons especially fear being dominated by or being overdependent on others and so are led by their fear to withdraw from their fellows and live too much in a private world of their own. Others are more afraid of finding themselves isolated from their fellows or excluded from their company, and so are led to pretend to opinions that they do not hold for fear of being rejected. Both these fears hinder self-realisation: the one fear turns a man into a timid non-participant, the other into an insincere conformist. A genuine faith will help each of these opposite types of person to overcome his fear. To the one it will give the courage to go out to others and be open and frank despite misgivings; to the other it will give the courage to declare his convictions, to say what he really thinks and feels and risk rejection. But the faith that enables a man to conquer his fear is a mature faith, and faith is often far from mature.

Idolatry and immaturity

It will make the meaning of immature faith clearer if we return to the subject of idolatry as it was interpreted in chapter 2 as the giving of absolute value to an object or idea of only relative worth. A man may give absolute value to money, for example. Money is useful, as everyone quickly discovers when he is short of it. One who gives supreme value to money regards it as his principal weapon against everything that threatens him as a person. It is an alternative to the risks he runs by being open to others and to his own depths. It is a protective device behind which the ego can shelter and so be relieved of the necessity of becoming mature. A man's home, family or friends or indeed his country can be given supreme value and everything subordinated to the idol on which he relies in order to feel secure. All these things are good in themselves, they become bad only when they are relied on as substitutes for relying on the God who meets him in people and events as well as in his own depths.

The peace of mind which a wise man will certainly value and to some extent guard can be made into an idol to which he is tempted to subordinate everything else. If he does this consistently he will endeavour to shrug off all duties and evade all claims that threaten his peace of mind. One of the effects of this would be to damage him as a person and prevent his growth to self-realisation; for it is impossible to fulfil yourself, to become mature while living in an ivory tower. Another unavoidable effect would be that in the end he would fail to preserve the peace of mind which he sought so assiduously; for idols have no power to protect either themselves or their worshippers.

To give absolute value to something of only relative worth is one kind of idolatry. But there is another kind more dangerous to the man who believes in God, the idolatry of giving supreme value to some idea identified with God or to some false image of God. It was partly because they were likely to lead to false ideas of God that the Bible condemns all material representations of the Godhead. No mental image or idea of God that the human mind can form is adequate to the reality of God. 'His thoughts are not our thoughts nor his ways our ways.' It is a commonplace of traditional theology that men can know *that* God is but not *what* he is. In some sense God must be the Unknown. The ideas we form of him are at best just pointers to a mystery that we can dimly sense but cannot grasp. Perhaps Jung's concept of the self provides the best image of the Godhead; for the self is by definition something that a man cannot grasp totally, though he is aware of it in part. He can make himself aware of his unconscious partly through reflecting on its effect on his conscious personality. It is this kind of indirect knowledge we have of the self, most of which is unconscious, that makes it a suggestive model for our thinking about God. Idols degrade our thinking about God also because they are man-made and therefore in some sense man's tools. A material image is made to be used and a mental image is equally a tool of the mind. To the genuine believer the idea of using God is a blasphemy.

The man who valued peace of mind above everything else might conceivably make an image to represent it as a kind of visual aid to assist concentration and reflection on the quality he loved. More likely he would have a vague mental idea of peace not explicitly formulated even to himself which would express his goal. A further case which is more relevant to the argument of this chapter would be that of the man who professes to believe in God, is perhaps a regular church-goer and yet looks upon God as simply and solely the guarantor of his peace. When he does fall prey to anxiety he either feels that God has let him down or that God is punishing him for some failure on his part. There are professing Christians who use their religion as an anaesthetic to deaden the pain or anxiety of life in this world or a sedative to help them to sleep through the troubles of those around them. There is a passage in the first letter of John where the writer speaks precisely of this kind of idolatry. 'If a man says that he loves God and hates his brother he is a liar' (1 John 4:20). John is not thinking here of a deliberate hypocrite, of a man who pretends to be religious in order to win the regard of his Christian friends. The man he has in mind believes that he loves God. He has an idea of God that is precious to him; it gives him a sense of peace and security; he loves the idea and would defend it hotly if attacked. But the real God is not an idea, so the Christian believes, but an active presence addressing him through his brother.

Two current false images of God

Two particular false conceptions of God deserve mention because of their prevalence today, not so much in explicitly formulated ideas but in uncriticised assumptions only partly conscious. One of these is of a father all-kind and all-tolerant but, alas, ineffective. The other is of a stern repressive father. As we have seen, the whole of our later life is coloured by the impressions we receive in infancy and childhood. It looks as though both these ideas of God have their roots in childhood experience of parents. They are perhaps related to the two kinds of parental love referred to earlier, the all-accepting love of mother and the demanding love of father, but each of them in an exaggerated form and lacking the correctives that the other would supply. A child who has lacked the all-accepting love of mother or the demanding love of father is apt to crave for these; and the craving is likely to colour whatever teaching he receives about God. Equally if he has suffered the too possessive love of mother or the too severe discipline of father he may come to reject God if he believes him to share these qualities.

Many a person's rejection of religion is in fact the rejection of either the kind, all-tolerant idea of God or the stern, repressive father idea. The first of these is rejected because in view of the harsh facts of life, of earthquake, famine, disease and war, such a God seems incredible. The second is rejected because it seems an affront to man's dignity and responsibility as a person. Neither of these ideas of God tallies with the traditional belief of either Christians, Jews or Moslems. They are mentioned because they hinder the growth both of a mature faith in God and of self-realisation. For only total self-commitment to God can be the adequate correlative and support to full self-acceptance. Inadequate ideas of God make this total self-commitment impossible. We cannot trust ourselves to the kind, all-tolerant God, because he is not in command and therefore cannot be relied on to see us through our difficulties. We cannot commit ourselves to the tyrannical God because to do so would be to reject part of our manhood.

I have pointed out in this chapter that the great obstacle to self-realisation is fear and have maintained that a mature faith can enable a person to overcome this obstacle. I have tried to show that the power of genuine faith has been obscured by various kinds of immature and childish faith. In a final brief chapter I shall sketch the kind of Christian belief

71

that will help those who hold to it to grow to their full stature as persons.

4

The relevance of belief today

Modern science and technology holds out new and exciting possibilities for the future of mankind. Man is becoming increasingly master of his environment. Modern hygiene and medicine have banished the plagues that used regularly to decimate cities and nations. Modern, scientific agriculture has got rid of the spectre of famine at least from those parts of the world that have been willing or able to adopt its methods. Television and jet travel have made possible a clearer and deeper appreciation by all men of the gifts and talents, the problems, the sufferings and the possibilities of every nation under the sun. Man has even learnt how to escape from the gravitational pull of the earth and touch down on the moon. There is a real possibility of a fuller and richer life for every inhabitant of the globe.

Yet for all these heart-warming possibilities men are everywhere anxious. The same technology that has given man the power to stand on the moon has given him the power to destroy all life on the earth. The hydrogen bomb, though it has never been used in war, nevertheless exists to set a question mark against the hope of a better future for man on this planet. Modern medicine and hygiene which have so much benefited mankind have brought about a rapid increase in the population of the world, which will pose great problems if famine and starvation are not to return on a scale vaster than ever before. The task of averting this calamity is by no means impossible, but it will demand co-operation and a sense of responsibility to a degree that has never been required of man before. Meanwhile, enormous sums are being spent annually by those nations that can afford it on armaments both offensive and defensive. It is not true that increased material prosperity of itself brings greater harmony either between nations or classes or even between individuals in the home. It tends to make the have-nots envious and the haves defensive. Mutual suspicion and fear divide a large part of the world into two great power blocks. The richest nation in the world is torn by fierce racial antagonism.

It may be that the anxieties and the antagonisms that are widespread today are the birth pangs of a new age, 'the time of tension between dying and birth'. What seems to be demanded of men as never before is a spirit of tolerance and the willingness to take the risk of trusting their fellows. These qualities are required between parents and their children, between man and man. In a word, what the state of the world demands today is greater maturity; and the great obstacle to this, as we have seen, is fear. It is here that belief in God is relevant, for faith is the supreme antidote to fear. The believer in the sovereignty of God, whether he be Moslem, Jew or Christian, can see the hand of God in the technological revolution that is changing the world and is challenging man to come of age. It may be that nothing but a revival of faith in God will be able to steady man's nerves and strengthen his hand for the task of using the rapidly expanding resources of science and technology to build a richer and a happier world.

The Christian faith in God

The time has come for believers of whatever religious tradition to close their ranks and co-operate with all who are prepared to work for greater maturity and tolerance among men. I believe that religions other that Christianity have important insights that are needed; and despite its ruthless subordination of individual and personal values to the interests of many, that the secular faith of communism has its contribution to make. But in this concluding chapter I must give my reasons for believing that the Christian way of relying on God is peculiarly relevant.

In chapter 3 I referred to two current false images of God, that of the all-kind, all-tolerant Father, and that of the stern, tyrannical God. The Christian believer finds in the man Jesus of Nazareth, the key both to his understanding of God and

74

to the true meaning of human life. The God of whom Jesus spoke, whom he made real to men, is neither all-tolerant nor tyrannical. The patience of God which looks like unlimited tolerance or heartless indifference is part of God's concern for man's freedom and his refusal to do for man what man could do for himself. The severity of God that looks like tyranny is his unrelenting opposition, like that of a doctor to the cancer that is destroying his patient, to all that diminishes and enslaves man. Jesus spoke of a loving Father whose demands cannot be evaded but who is also completely trustworthy. He was outlining the true life of man when he said, 'Don't worry about food and drink and dress; put God first and these other things will take care of themselves' (see Matthew 6:31–3). Complete loyalty to God and unanxious trust in him will set a man free from all other cares. For Jesus fear and distrust of God were the great enemies. To quote Harry Williams:

> If you want to discover the difference which Jesus made to mankind, and go to the New Testament to find out, the answer given is the casting out of people's lives of fear. Fear, in the New Testament, is considered to be the root of all evil. It is fear which makes men selfish, it is fear which makes them hate, it is fear which makes them blind, it is fear which makes them mad. Fear casts out love, as love casts out fear.[1]

Jesus not only taught this, he lived it. He declared the true life of man to be one of complete loyalty to God and total trust in him, which if genuine would overflow inevitably in a life of openness to and trust in others. He tells his disciples to give to those who ask from them, to lend without expectation of return. He tells them to love their enemies, to do good to their persecutors, to pray for those who ill use them. All this sounds hopelessly unpractical. If I gave to all who asked I might not only reduce myself to poverty but encourage others to become cadgers and scroungers. No doubt Jesus was a poet and he was describing a spirit rather

[1] H. A. Williams, *The True Wilderness* (Fount, 1979), p. 66.

than outlining a programme of action. But the spirit of the sermon on the mount was the way that he actually lived.

Although Christians have always officially believed in the genuine humanity of Christ they have often spoken and written as though he were physically human but psychologically divine. They have supposed that unlike other men he could see clearly into the future and know in advance all that would follow from his words and actions. New Testament scholarship has helped us to recognise anew the completeness of his humanity, to see him as a man of his times, a Jew of the first century, sharing most of the ideas of his fellow Jews, including some which we now regard as mistaken. Perhaps it was because he was able to respond so completely to the needs and demands of his own times that he is able to be the man for all time. It would seem that it was his total reliance on God that enabled him to accept the whole of what he was, and this total acceptance of himself enabled him to appreciate and love other people as they were: the socially disreputable and those notorious for their easy morals, as well as simple fishermen, strict-living religious people or subtle lawyers. He cut through social conventions and so made enemies of those who relied on convention to maintain the social *status quo* or buttress their own self-esteem. He held the crowds spell-bound by the authority of experience out of which he spoke and the down-to-earth quality of the stories by which he explained the meaning of life. His popularity with the crowds made him the suspect of the Romans who feared a rising and the enemy of the Jewish authorities who feared the undermining of their own influence. The inevitable, which he foresaw, yet did nothing to avoid, happened. He was arrested, condemned to death and executed like a common criminal.

It looked like the end. This is what happens to a man who tries to live authentically, to be true to what he knows, to rely totally on God, in a world which fears authenticity and regards God as bound up with the established order. But it was not the end. His disciples were convinced that he had risen from the dead and spent the rest of their lives declaring the news of it. Somehow through Christ's resurrection and his presence with them, as they believed, they found them-

76

selves largely set free from the fears that held them back from complete commitment to God and their fellows. Through Christ they discovered themselves, they were new men, they were free and unafraid, they were beginning to live with something of the openness and integrity of Christ. The Christian explanation of this is that God was uniquely present in Christ showing men how to be fully human, disclosing to men both his own character and what men have it in them to become.

Faith and community

Some words that St Luke ascribes to Jesus give an apt description of the impact he has made on the world: 'I came to cast fire on the earth and would that it were already kindled.' Fire is something both beneficent and dangerous. Jesus himself resembled fire and there is a saying early attributed to him though not found in any of the gospels: 'He that is near me is near fire.' Jesus had seemed a destructive threat to the Jewish authorities. His total reliance on God, his freedom from the fears and anxieties that belittle most men, his courage and integrity, his openhearted love for his fellow men, especially the unpopular and disreputable, was a disclosure of the meaning of human life, a revelation of what man can be. But it constituted a threat to the old order. His new way of living made the old look shabby by comparison; men and women were drawn to it as by a magnet; others were beginning to catch fire from him. His execution was an attempt to put out the fire. But his enemies found that it had broken out again among his disciples who were unshakably convinced that Jesus had risen from the dead and was alive. The infectious boldness and freedom from anxiety that they had noted in Jesus was present in the company of the disciples centred round the apostles in Jerusalem. In a few years the fire had spread far and wide over the Roman world, partly as a result of the persecution designed to put it out. In communities of varying size dotted round the shores of the Mediterranean men were to be found living with something of the quality of life that had been disclosed in Jesus.

It is necessary to look at the origin of the Christian movement, for it is there that its nature is most clearly seen. As a bright bonfire is damped down when a mass of sodden leaves or damp branches is heaped on it, so the original fire of the Christian spirit was obscured first when the Roman empire ceased to persecute and became officially Christian, and later after the collapse of the empire when the barbarian nations of Europe became nominally Christian. Christianity became the inspiration of the medieval European civilisation to which our modern world is heir. But with all the gains that this has meant for mankind the fire that first burned brilliantly in Palestine has been dimmed, though its smouldering embers are very much alive and are constantly liable to burst into flame.

Jesus Christ is the centre of Christian belief. The Christian believes that the character of the God who is all the time addressing him (and all other men) through the world of people outside him and through his own depths has been disclosed in Christ. It is a Christ-coloured faith in God that enables the Christian to overcome the fears that hinder self-realisation. I mention two ways in which the Christian is helped to grow into a mature faith: through the fellowship of a believing community and through corporate worship.

The first disciples found themselves bound together by their shared faith in God and their shared loyalty to Christ. It was the faith of a community, of a believing brotherhood, that enabled its individual members to grow out of the fears that hindered their self-realisation into a new freedom. In the community of faith a man felt accepted for what he was and in spite of what he was. The basis of the fellowship of Alcoholics Anonymous is the acknowledging by the members of their common weakness and the discarding of all pretence to be stronger than they are. In that society the alcoholic no longer needs to act a part and is helped to realise himself more completely as a person. Similarly the shared belief of the first Christians that the God made known to them in Jesus Christ had accepted them as they were and in spite of what they were, enabled them to accept themselves and so to accept others. The phrase, the peace of God, which recurs like a refrain in St Paul's letters, refers to this realis-ation of God's acceptance which overflowed in a spirit of love and acceptance towards others. In this fellowship men and women, regardless of differences of race, education and social position found themselves free and at one. In the first days of the Christian Church the brotherhood of Christians both within the local community and in the sense of membership in a great and widely scattered body, was a powerful reality. 'We know', writes St John, 'that we have passed out of death into life because we love the brethren.'

These first Christians were very far from perfect, as St Paul's letters make clear. Whether their background had been Jewish or pagan, the new life within the Church did not at once eradicate all the old habits and ways of thinking. There were scandals and there were quarrels. Indeed in any genuinely free society there is bound to be sharp disagreement sometimes. But they were people who had undergone, no doubt with varying degrees of intensity, the experience of liberation. Their faith had enabled them to realise themselves as never before and given them a hope that was transforming their lives. It is within the context of the shared faith of a community, that is of the Church, that individual faith becomes fully intelligible.

Faith and worship

One of the ways in which the first Christians were freed from fear and discovered themselves was through their membership in a believing community. This community faith is expressed in worship. We have seen how idolatrous worship can keep men immature by helping them to repress aspects of themselves of which they are afraid or disapprove. At its best the worship of the Church is the surest corrective of the idolatry of false or inadequate ideas of God. The corporate worship of the Church with its readings from the Scriptures, especially when these are interpreted in the light of Jesus Christ and in the language of today, provides an escape from narrow and ego-centric ideas of God into the larger faith of the community. Worship, as the derivation of the word (from worth-ship) implies, means declaring what we value most. A man declares what he values in other ways than the formal worship that goes on in a church building: he declares it by the things he does and the way he does them, by the way he treats other people, by the way he accepts good fortune and bad. A man's values will reveal themselves in his whole life. In the formal worship of the Church men orient and correct their values. William Temple expressed this when he said, 'It is not that conduct is the end of life and worship helps it, but that worship is the end of life and conduct tests it.' A man's conduct will show what he really values. Most people have more than one set of values; the worship of God should strengthen the highest, that is the most fully human values.

The meaning of worship as the expressing, correcting and orienting of the believer's values is best seen in the corporate action called the Eucharist or the Lord's Supper. What is done there finds its meaning in Christ once crucified but now, so Christians believe, alive and present. In the Eucharist the believer affirms his conviction of the value of truth, justice, courage, generosity and compassion not in the abstract but embodied in a man. In Christ is set forth both the character of God and the meaning of human commitment. The commitment of faith means involving ourselves in the world of men and women which God created and loves. It means taking the risk of relying on our own depths, on other people, on the way things happen. We don't need to be starry eyed and unrealistic and to suppose that we shall never be let down if we open ourselves to others in this way. Christ made himself vulnerable and suffered in consequence. The crucifixion of Christ has placed the possibility of being let down at the heart of the Christian's faith. But behind the ignorance, fear, selfishness and folly of men God is at work, so Christians believe, bringing good out of evil, turning tragedy into triumph. After the cross came the resurrection; behind death there is life. In the Eucharist the death and resurrection of Christ are celebrated. In one of the Eucharistic liturgies in current use, after the thanksgiving prayer, the president says the words, 'Let us proclaim the mystery of faith', and the people respond: 'Christ has died, Christ is risen, Christ will come again.' In the Eucharist the Christian man orients his values; he sets his compass by Christ.

In this brief and incomplete sketch of Christian belief,

community and worship I have been describing an ideal which is very imperfectly realised in practice. There is a great gap between the Church as it is with its divisions, its small-mindedness, its often irrelevant worship and the Church of God's design, a brotherhood of believers in which men are strengthened and liberated to face the tasks of mankind in today's world. All the same there is a new spirit abroad and great changes are on the way. There is growing self-criticism among Christians and decreasing self-satisfaction. It may be that the glowing embers of the fire that Christ lit will once again burst into a great flame. To name only three signs of the renewal that is taking place, there is the movement for co-operation and ultimate union between the different denominations of Christians; there is the liturgical movement affecting Christians of every confession with its concern for a worship in which all men can participate with under-standing, and there is the growing concern of Christians for justice in the world.

This book has tried to show how depth psychology can shed light both on religious experience and on the import-ance of the factor of faith in man's growth to maturity. In the final chapter I have tried to suggest how Christian faith can help those who hold to it to a fuller self-realisation. I have not tried to prove the truth of Christian belief. Because a belief is helpful it is not necessarily true. Ultimately the question of the truth or falsehood of the Christian vision of reality is more important than that of its relevance or irrel-evance. But here and now most people appear to think religion irrelevant, and so the question of its truth or false-hood hardly comes up for consideration. To show that it matters, that it could in fact make a great and beneficial difference to its adherents, that it might help them to realise themselves more fully as persons, is the first step to getting many people to consider it at all. But if religious belief can lead men to a fuller and more meaningful life it may be worth while looking seriously at the question, could it be true?

Further reading

The following list, selected from a vast literature, is specially relevant to Christopher Bryant's approach. In addition to his own publications which develop themes introduced in this book, there are some which were valued and referred to by him in his writings, and others which are consistent with and amplify his psychological formulations. Four general overviews may be of value in approaching the psychology of religion (Faber, Spinks), psychotherapy and mechanisms of defence (Brown and Pedder), and the thought and practice of C. G. Jung (Fordham).

Bryant, C., *The River Within*. Darton Longman and Todd 1978.

Bryant, C., *The Heart in Pilgrimage*. Darton Longman and Todd 1980.

Bryant, C., *Jung and the Christian Way*. Darton Longman and Todd 1983.

Brown, D. and Pedder, J., *Introduction to Psychotherapy*. Tavistock 1979.

Faber, H., *The Psychology of Religion*. SCM 1972.

Fordham, F., *An Introduction to Jung's Psychology*. Penguin 1953.

Hobson, R. F., *Forms of Feeling: the Heart of Psychotherapy*. Tavistock 1985.

James, W., *The Varieties of Religious Experience*. Longmans Green 1947.

Jung, C. G., *Modern Man in Search of a Soul*. Routledge 1933.

Jung, C. G., *Memories, Dreams and Reflections*. Fontana 1967.

Spinks, G. S., *Psychology and Religion*. Methuen 1963.

Storr, A., *The Integrity of the Personality*. Penguin 1970.

White, V., *God and the Unconscious*. Harvill Press 1952.